Banking and Finance Series

QUESTIONS AND ANSWERS ON

Practice of Banking (Part 1)

Banking and Finance Series

QUESTIONS AND ANSWERS ON
Practice of Banking (Part 1)

by

Michael Marsden A.I.B.

Bank of Credit and Commerce International, London

Graham & Trotman

First published in 1985 by

Graham & Trotman Limited
Sterling House
66 Wilton Road
London SW1V 1DE

Graham & Trotman Inc.
13 Park Avenue
Gaithersburg
MD 20877, USA

© Michael Marsden, 1985

ISBN 978-0-86010-588-6

This publication is protected by International Copyright Law. All rights reserved. No part of this publication may be reproduced, stored in a retrieval system, or transmitted in any form or by any means, electronic, mechanical, photocopying, recording or otherwise, without the prior permission of the copyright holder.

Typeset in Great Britain by The Castlefield Press, Northants

Contents

	Series Foreword	vii
	Introduction	ix
Section 1	Banker/Customer Relationship	1
Section 2	Bankruptcy	9
Section 3	Types of Account	16
Section 4	Executors and Administrators	29
Section 5	The Paying and Collecting Banker	33
Section 6	Security for Advances	39
Section 7	Security for Advances (cont.)	47
Section 8	Security for Advances (cont.)	52
Section 9	Security for Advances (cont.)	58
Section 10	Further Examination Questions	62
	Answers	
	Section 1	67
	Section 2	73
	Section 3	79
	Section 4	89
	Section 5	93

Section 6 ... 97
Section 7 ... 103
Section 8 ... 107
Section 9 ... 112
Section 10 ... 115

Series Foreword

The *Banking and Finance Series* has been written for students who are preparing for the Associateship of the Institute of Bankers. The structure of the series follows the syllabus closely. Although the emphasis is on the Institute of Bankers' examinations the series is also relevant to students for the kinds of other professional examinations such as the different Accountancy Bodies, Chartered Secretaries, Diploma in Public Administration, undergraduate business course, B.T.E.C., B.E.C., H.N.D., D.M.S., Stock Exchange courses, Association and Corporate Treasurers, Institute of Freight Forwarders, Institute of Export.

August 1985

Brian Kettell
Series Editor

Introduction

This Question and Answer Revision Guide has been compiled with a view to it being used either in conjunction with the textbook on *Practice of Banking, Part 1*, which is also published by Graham and Trotman, or as a separate *aide mémoire* and revision tool for the Institute of Bankers examination in this subject.

The guide consists of ten sections and by and large the contents of each section correspond to the topics covered in the relative and similarly-numbered chapter of the textbook. There is, however, some overlap since the questions and model answers are based substantially on past examination questions, and sometimes their content necessitates straddling the guide sections and textbook chapters.

Each section takes the form of headings, sub-headings and brief tabulated information on the topic concerned, with references where appropriate to relevant Case and Statute law. Specimen questions are interspersed, with the specimen answers being given at the end of the book. The questions are graded in order of difficulty and readers are recommended to attempt their own answer before looking at the suggested answers provided in the latter part of the book.

Questions are graded A, B, or C, with A being those considered the most difficult, B moderately difficult and C least difficult.

Section 1

Banker/Customer Relationship

- Definition of "banker" and "customer.".
- Banking Act 1979:
  - Background to and aim of legislation.
  - Authorisation as Recognised Bank or Licensed Deposit Taking Institution.
  - Different aspects of Banker/Customer Relationship:

(1) CONTRACTUAL
(*JOACHIMSON V. SWISS BANK CORPORATION* (1921))

Involves *duty of secrecy*; this qualified by conditions in *Tournier v. National Provincial Bank* (1924) as follows:

- Under Compulsion by law.
- Under a Public Duty.
- Where interests of bank require disclosure
- With customer's express or implicit consent.
- *Status Enquiries* — dangers involved in replying and practical considerations.

Question 1

How would you deal with the following two requests?:

(a) In the last two weeks several cheques payable to local tradesmen have been presented at your branch signed "A. Johnson". As they did not bear the usual signature of your customer, A. Johnson, the cheques were returned by your branch marked "Drawer's signature requires confirmation." You now receive a visit from a police officer who is making investigations on behalf of the local tradespeople. He asks you for the full name and address of the customer to whom you issued the cheque book and also whether you can throw any further light on the matter.

[B]

(b) You have been informed that your customer, Eric Edwards, has been arrested by the police and you have now seen confirmation of this in your local paper. The newspaper states that Edwards is being held in custody on charges of fraud. A police officer calls on you a few days later and requests copies of Edwards' statements over the past two years. He indicates to you that the charges against Edwards are very serious ones and says that the statements will be needed for the Court proceedings.

[B]

Question 2

How would you deal with the following situations and requests?

(a) Mr. Tom Wyatt opened his current and deposit accounts 18 months ago. Shortly afterwards, he wrote giving strict instructions that you should not answer any enquiries, including requests for bankers' opinions, which you might receive. Whilst you were surprised at this, you agreed, in view of the substantial balances on the accounts. You have now received a letter from the Inland Revenue asking you to supply a copy of all bank accounts in Mr. Wyatt's name covering the period from the time the accounts were opened to date. The letter also asks you to forward all paid cheques to the Inland Revenue and to supply a list of all securities held by the bank for Mr. Wyatt.

[C]

(b) One of your larger and important company customers, is intending to make arrangements for the payment of the salaries of its 350 staff into current accounts in their names to be opened at your branch. Before they progress this idea, they are seeking to ascertain how many of their staff already have accounts of any sort with you. The company secretary produces a list of the staff of the company and asks you to indicate on the list which names are known to you as already being customers.

[C]

(2) DEBTOR/CREDITOR RELATIONSHIP

This part of the Banker/Customer relationship itself has several angles:

APPROPRIATION OF PAYMENTS

- by (firstly) the debtor, or (secondly) the creditor, or (if neither debtor nor creditor has appropriated) by the law (Rule in Clayton's Case — *Devaynes v. Noble* (1816))
- practical aspects involve earmarking of credits by customer to meet specific cheques, or to cover debit interest to enable relative tax certificate to be given.
- appropriation by operation of Rule in Clayton's Case very important and a current account may need to be broken if it is necessary to prevent the Rule operating to a bank's detriment.

SET OFF

- right of banker to combine or set-off the various accounts of a customer to determine the net balance due to or from the customer.

- Accounts in the same name and same right.
- Not current accounts and loan accounts.
- Set-off acquired by express agreement (but not where trust monies involved).
- Automatic right of set off — on death, liquidation or bankruptcy.

Question 3

Robert Ball maintains a No. 1 account and a No. 2 account at your branch. His No. 1 account is overdrawn from time to time but the position has deteriorated over the last two months and the present balance is debit £1300.

Over the last 10 months regular payments have been made into the No. 2 account and this account is now credit £1600.

Additionally, Ball has a partnership account with his brother, which has a present balance of credit £1900.

You have written to Ball asking him for his proposals for dealing with the overdraft on his No. 1 account. You have suggested to him that he should make a transfer either from the No. 2 account or from the partnership account to clear the No. 1 account indebtedness.

He calls to see you and states that he has no financial interest in the partnership account at all; he had become partner to be available in case his brother, who is 10 years older and in poor health, should die. The balance on the No. 2 account is held by Ball as secretary of a travel association and is being collected for a holiday trip to Europe by the members. He will shortly pay the travel agent for the trip with a cheque for £1600 drawn on the No. 2 account. State, with reasons, what course of action you would now take in dealing with Ball's accounts. Could the bank have taken any earlier action to prevent this position arising.?

[B]

JOINT AND SEVERAL LIABILITY

- *joint liability* — action against one party even if unsuccessful prevents action against other party(ies). Death of one debtor leaves creditor with sole recourse against survivor(s). No right of set-off accrues over credit balance of individual against debt for which he is jointly liable with others.
- *joint and several liability* — creditor has as many rights of action as there are debtors. An unsatisfied judgement against one does not bar action against other(s). Estate of a deceased joint debtor remains liable (but account must be stopped re Clayton's Case). Private accounts can be set-off against the joint debt, but arguably notice needed.

ENTRIES ON BANK STATEMENTS

- law on this aspect of banking not particularly clear. When error on account discovered by bank, it should quickly be ascertained whether the incorrect balance has been communicated to the customer. If so, customer must be contacted quickly so that hopefully he will not have changed his position relying on the incorrect statement. Points to watch are:
  - *Customer overcredited* — may draw cheques in reliance on the inflated balance and bank may have to honour these.

- *Cheques not debited* — not so serious as customer should know what cheques are still to be presented.
- *Customer undercredited* — have any cheques been returned and customer's credit damaged wrongly?
- *Cheque debited in error* — again have any cheques been wrongly returned because of this?

Question 4

You have for several years been transferring under standing order the sum of £350 per month from the account of your customer A. Cox to his wife's account at another branch. Almost six months ago, Cox wrote informing you that he and his wife had separated and he instructed you not to make any further payments. Due to an oversight in your standing order department, your branch did not cancel the standing order and thus £1750 has been paid out of Mr. Cox's account after you had received his instructions to cease the payments. A statement has been sent to him every month and he today calls in to see you to complain that the last five payments should not have been made.

Discuss the bank's position as regards both Mr. Cox and his wife.

[C]

LIEN

The right of one person to retain something that is in his possession belonging to another until certain demands by the person in possession are satisfied.

- *Particular Lien* — when the right to retain is over the goods in connection with which the debt arose.
- *General Lien* — the right to retain goods not only in connection with which the debt arose but for the general balance outstanding from the owner.
- *Banker's Lien* — general lien on all securities deposited with them in the ordinary course of banking business by or on behalf of their customers in respect of any balance that may be due from such customer. No lien arises if there is an implied or express contract to the contrary. Banker's lien gives banker right to realise and recoup himself from proceeds of negotiable securities.

Question 5

Explain and give an example of the following:

1. Particular lien.   2. General lien.   3. Banker's lien.

Would a bank have a lien on

(i) Deeds left accidentally on the bank counter, by a customer, when he called to pay in a credit.
(ii) Securities left at the bank, by a customer, with oral instructions that the bank should retain them as security in respect of the customer's overdraft.
(iii) Securities left at the bank by a customer, for safe custody? Give reasons for your answers to (i), (ii) and (iii).

[B]

BANKER/CUSTOMER RELATIONSHIP

GARNISHEE ORDERS AND INJUNCTIONS

- banker's contract to repay on demand is determined by operation of law. Garnishee Order is order of the court obtained by judgement creditor attaching funds in the hands of a third party which are owed to the judgement debtor.

Two stages to garnishee proceedings

- service of garnishee order nisi: is served on garnishee (i.e. person holding the funds) and requires him to hold for discharge of the debt and costs all funds in his hands owing to judgement debtor.
- then follows making the order absolute: this directs actual payment over from the frozen funds.
- Garnishee Summons — similar to order nisi but gives garnishee the option of paying into Court sufficient to satisfy the debt and costs. This frees any surplus funds in the garnishee's hands.

Balances attached:

- Current Accounts — banker can firstly exercise any right of set-off. Only attaches funds in hands of bank at time of service.
- Deposit and Savings Accounts.
- NOT joint accounts unless all parties are quoted in order as judgement debtors.
- Partnership Accounts — attached if the judgement debtor is the partnership; not if one or more partners is judgement debtor.
- Trust Accounts — may still be caught by order. Solicitor's Client's account can be — *Plunkett v. Barclays Bank Ltd* (1936). Bank must advise Court of nature of trust and advise customer immediately that the account is frozen.

Practical Steps:

- Stop Account(s) and advise customer. If garnishee for limited amount this can be isolated and customer can deal with remainder of balance.
- Place subsequent credits to new account.
- Ascertain attached balance — deduct uncleared effects, exercise any right of set-off and deduct any amount for which bank committed e.g. purchase of shares via Stock Exchange on customer's behalf.
- If no funds to be attached, advise creditor's solicitor accordingly.

"Mareva" Injunctions — this type of injunction has reared its head over recent years and basically is an order sought by a creditor before judgement; the order being to prevent the debtor from disposing of assets before legal proceedings. The growing use of this type of order, which did not relate merely to bank balances, caused severe practical difficulties to banks and these were recognised in recent law cases, which resulted in certain restrictions being placed on the effect of this type of injunction.

(3) PRINCIPAL/AGENT RELATIONSHIP

Law of Agency relevant to bankers as banks act as agents for customers and also have normal business transactions with customers acting as agents — e.g. partners, directors, "per pro" signatures on cheques.

Agent need not have full contractual capacity as he is not contracting on his own behalf — thus minor and undischarged bankrupts can act as agents (there are statutory restrictions on some aspects of undischarged bankrupt's activities which would limit his right to act).

Agent can be appointed:

- by deed — Power of Attorney.
- in writing
- orally (obviously would not be accepted by banks)
- by estoppel or implication
- by ratification.
- by necessity

Authority of Agent:

- may be expressed in writing or implied by circumstances of case e.g. partner in trading firm has implied authority to borrow on behalf of firm.

Rights and Duties of Agent:

- must exercise due diligence and use any special skills he professes to have.
- must not delegate his authority — maxim *delegatus non potest delegare.* Exceptions to this are where custom sanctions delegation; where there is statutory, express or implied authority to delegate; where it is necessary to delegate (e.g. banker using stockbroker); or where emergency dictates the employing of a substitute.
- agent entitled to his agreed renumeration (thus banker entitled to charge interest and commission)
- agent entitled to be indemnified by principal for acts properly and lawfully done whilst acting as agent.
- the principal may have to acknowledge an equitable right of a lender acting on good faith when the agent has borrowed money without or in excess of his authority. This equity can protect agent who pays his principal's debts without authority — this can be of practical significance to a bank if it pays cheques which are not drawn in accordance with mandate but which pay off genuine debts of customer thereby not changing amount of customer's liabilities — *Liggett v. Barclays Bank Ltd* (1928).

Agency terminated:

- by renunciation on part of agent or revocation by principal (when agency revoked, third parties may need to be informed — e.g. if partner leaves firm he may still be liable for debts incurred after retirement if he ostensibly remains a member. Similarly with a joint account where it is either to sign, if the banker hears of a dispute between the parties he should regard mandate as cancelled and insist on both signatures).
- Death, mental disorder or bankruptcy of principal terminates agency.
- Death and mental disorder of agent similarly terminates agency but not necessarily his bankruptcy.
- Agency can also be terminated by the expiration of a certain time or when a particular purpose fulfilled.

Mandates and Powers of Attorney.

- *Mandate* — does not itself delegate powers but is advice of delegation with request to accept agent's instructions as set out.
- *Power of Attorney* — is actual instrument embodying authorisation. Powers of

Attorney Act 1971 simplified dealing with powers of attorney by prescribing a form of general power of attorney which gave the donee authority to do on behalf of the donor anything that the donor himself could lawfully do. Banker needs to exercise care where private account of an attorney is under pressure to ensure that attorney not permitted to abuse power for own benefit — *Midland Bank Ltd. v. Reckitt & Others* (1933).

(4) BAILMENT — BAILOR/BAILEE RELATIONSHIP

Bailment is delivery of goods on express or implied condition that they be returned by bailee to bailor when purpose for which they were bailed is fulfilled.

- Banker holding goods for safe custody is acting as bailee (is like a warehouseman) and no property in the goods passes to the banker.
- Difference between paid and gratuitous bailees is nowadays not very clear cut since the same safeguards will be adopted by bank irrespective of whether specific charge being made for safe custody service.
- If goods destroyed, lost or stolen, bank is liable if there has been negligence on its part.
- Goods held must be returned to depositor and no one else unless on depositor's clear instructions. If reasonable doubt exists about authenticity of instructions, it is advisable to delay release pending confirmation.
- Authority to deliver to third parties is cancelled on death of depositor when legal personal representatives must give discharge; in the case of mental disorder the appointed Receiver or Court of Protection are only people who can deal with the items.
- In the event of bankruptcy the Official Receiver or Trustee in Bankruptcy can give a good discharge.

Question 6

You are holding for safe custody certain share certificates on behalf of your customer Mr. Bennett. The share certificates are in the name of Mr. Bennett's nephew and the nephew calls to say that he knows the certificates are held by you and he asks you to hand them out to him.

How would you reply and why?

[C]

Question 7

Your customer Rogers has a locked tin box in safe custody at your branch and he sends his secretary to the bank with a letter authorising her to have access to the box in order to list the contents. Subsequently Rogers alleges that the secretary removed a valuable diamond brooch from the box and that she has now disappeared. Rogers claims that the bank is liable for restitution and damages.

What points would you consider in dealing with that claim? Do you think it might succeed?

[B]

Question 8

Your customer Barber asks if you will accept for safe custody a sealed envelope (contents unknown) with instructions that on his death the envelope is to be handed to his friend, Jones.

Would you be willing to accept and act upon these instructions? Give reasons for your answer.

[C]

Section 2

Bankruptcy

Bankruptcy is the compulsory winding up of the estate of a person who cannot pay his debts and its equitable distribution amongst his creditors.

Any person who has the capacity to contract may be made bankrupt.

Steps in bankruptcy process:
- Commission of available act of bankruptcy
- presentation of petition
- making of receiving order
- meeting of creditors
- public examination
- order of adjudication
- discharge

Acts of Bankruptcy:
- Assignment of whole of debtor's property for benefit of creditors generally
- Fraudulent Conveyance (important to bankers — In *re Simms* (1930).)
- Fraudulent Preference i.e. a payment or transfer of property made by a debtor when insolvent in favour of a creditor for the purpose of giving that creditor or any surety or guarantor an advantage over other creditors (Section 44 Bankruptcy Act 1914) Fraudulent Preferences are void as against Trustee but he must prove that the payment was made voluntarily with intention to prefer, it was made within 6 months of petition and debtor was insolvent when preference made. There must be intention to prefer, the mere fact that a creditor is preferred is not sufficient.

Re M. Kushler Ltd (1943).

Re William Hall (Contractors) Ltd (1967)

Re F.L.E. Holdings Ltd (1967).

Trustee may be able to recover from person to whom payment was made (e.g. a bank) even if this was not the person preferred.
- Keeping House — this is keeping out of way of creditors in an effort to defeat or delay.

- Seizure of goods by sheriff after execution has been levied.
- Bankruptcy petition presented by debtor himself.
- Bankruptcy Notice served on debtor to pay a judgement debt.
- Debtor giving notice to creditors of suspension of payment of debts.
- The making of an Administration Order.
- The making of a criminal bankruptcy order.

The Petition — can be presented by debtor himself or by a creditor owed £750 or more. Hearing takes place shortly after presentation and petition is either dismissed or a receiving order is made.

Receiving Order — constitutes Official Receiver of district receiver of the debtor's property. Debtor has to produce statement of affairs for creditors' meeting.

Creditors meeting — debtor may put forward scheme of arrangement which must normally offer minimum 25p in £ and must be approved by a majority in number and three quarters in value of the creditors. If sanctioned, Court rescinds receiving order. If not, then creditors elect a Trustee in Bankruptcy and in some cases a Committee of Inspection.

Public Examination — may take place but can be dispensed with under Insolvency Act 1976.

Adjudication Order — this declares the debtor bankrupt and his property now vests in Trustee who is empowered to sell assets for benefit of creditors as a whole.

Discharge — procedure now simplified by the automatic discharge rulings introduced by the Insolvency Act 1976.

Reputed Ownership — the Bankruptcy Act 1914 includes among the property divisible amongst creditors all goods which at the commencement of the bankruptcy were with the debtor in his trade or business, by consent and permission of true owner, under such circumstances that debtor is the reputed owner of them. This clause is to protect creditors from consquences of false credit a person may be given due to his having, as apparent owner, goods which did not belong to him. The true owner's only remedy would be to prove as an unsecured creditor for the value of the goods.

Question 9

A.B., a director and principal shareholder of XYZ Ltd., was surety for the company's account at the City Bank which for a number of years had permitted borrowing facilities to the company up to £800.

The bank knew that the company was experiencing difficulty in meeting its monthly accounts. Nevertheless between the 10th May and the 12th June, sufficient credits were paid into the account to place it in credit (for the first time in many years) and the covering security was released to the director at his request, the limit being cancelled.

During that period, save for two small sums, no trade payments were made out of the account.

It subsequently transpired, when a liquidator was appointed:

(i) That in the early part of May the Company's accountants had advised A.B. that the company was insolvent and would have to be wound up;

BANKRUPTCY

(ii) That on the 8th June, when the account was still slightly overdrawn, a resolution for voluntary winding up was passed but no notice of the Creditors' Meeting was sent to the bank.

(iii) That at the Creditors' Meeting A.B. suppressed the fact that he had been a guarantor for the Company's account.

Discuss the rights of (a) the liquidator (b) the bank.

[B]

Relation Back — Section 37 Bankruptcy Act 1914 stipulates that bankruptcy deemed to have commenced at time of first provable act of bankruptcy within 3 months preceding presentation of petition. This section exists because if the Trustee merely obtained what belonged to the bankrupt at the date of adjudication the debtor would have taken good care to divest himself of as much of his property as possible before he failed.

Protected Transactions — these are necessary to alleviate the considerable hardships that could face some parties if the doctrine of "relation back" was not tempered in favour of those who had entered into transactions with the debtor with no knowledge that an act of bankruptcy had been committed.

Two sections important to bankers:

- Section 45 — protects bona fide transactions with a bankrupt in ordinary course of business provided there "is no notice" of an act of bankruptcy and before a Receiving Order has been made.
(Section 45 will not give protection in the case of fraudulent preference)
- Section 46 — protects any payment or delivery to a bankrupt or his assignee provided it is without notice of presentation of a petition and before a Receiving Order has been made.

This Section raises the question of whether third party cheques are protected but the position remains unclear.

With credit accounts:

- Payments only to customer himself against existing balance.
- Subsequent credits to suspense account for 3 months in case claimed by Trustee.

With overdrawn accounts:

- Pay no cheques as additional overdraft created will not be provable against estate. Any "surplus" security cannot be relied on as it may be claimed by the Trustee under Relation Back.
- Securities — articles held for safe custody can be handed direct to customer but not to third parties.
- After notice of presentation of petition, no transactions must be permitted nor must any securities be released.
- After Receiving Order, the Official Receiver (or eventually the Trustee) alone may give good discharge.

Question 10

Your customer, J. Gray, has banked with you for some years and maintained good balances. You are therefore surprised to notice that a judgement for £900 has been made against him. On enquiry, Gray tells you he is involved in a dispute over a bill for £900 for house repairs and did not bother to attend Court in respect of the action on the debt. He did intend, however, to satisfy the judgement in due course.

Four weeks later you are formally advised that a receiving order has been made against Gray.

The balance on the account is £3600 credit.

You write to Gray who calls to see you the following day. He states that he was sent abroad by his firm urgently and was unable to attend to his affairs. He had not appreciated the situation regarding the unpaid bill for £900.

State how you would deal with the following, giving reasons for your decisions.

(a) There is a cheque in the clearing for £340 dated 10 days ago.

(b) Gray now urgently requires to cash a cheque for £150 to meet normal living expenses.

(c) His monthly salary £1250 is paid by credit to his bank and should arrive in the next two or three days.

(d) You hold a standing order to pay from his salary £320 to the account of Mrs. Gray (for housekeeping).

(e) From the date of the notice of the judgement to the making of the receiving order, cheques to a total of £440 have been paid from the account; this includes cash paid to either Gray or his wife to a total of £180.

[B]

Question 11

On 25th January, D. Hall, whose banking account was then Cr £960 (Marketable Shares value £800 also held under Memorandum of Deposit) advised one of his creditors that he was about to suspend payment of his debts. On 5th February notice of this came to his bank and on 23rd April a Receiving Order was made against Hall and the bank was immediately advised of this. Discuss the conduct of Hall's account from 15th January onwards giving full reasons for any action which you feel the bank should have taken.

If D. Hall's account had been overdrawn throughout the period, should the banker's action have differed in any way?

[B]

Question 12

Mr. Moore maintained a current account at the bank to which was credited his monthly salary of £860. The account had been opened 6 years ago and had of late proved hard to control. The bank was aware that Mr. Moore owed money to hire purchase companies and to credit card companies and in view of the call that these made upon his monthly salary, the bank had recently refused to grant him an advance. Following this, two cheques would have been returned to retailers had they not been drawn under his cheque card. The branch threatened to withdraw the banker's card, whereupon Mr. Moore promised to conduct his account properly and indeed a fortnight ago his account had a credit balance of £900 following receipt of his monthly salary. However, on that day the branch received notice of a receiving

BANKRUPTCY

order dated that day from the Official Receiver and the branch therefore froze the account and advised the balance of Cr £900 to him as requested. The following day cheques totalling £500 were presented through the clearing, each cheque having been issued to retailers in conjunction with Mr. Moore's cheque card. The branch took the view that, as payment had been guaranteed by the bank, it would have to pay the cheques. Moreover, as the cheques were all dated and issued prior to the date of the receiving order, it was felt that the bank should have to account to the Official Receiver only for the reduced balance of £400. Thus the cheques were paid and debited to Mr. Moore's account, with the Official Receiver being advised accordingly. The Official Receiver has objected to the suggestion that he should receive less than the £900 that was available at the time the receiving order was made and insists on claiming the whole sum.

What is your view of this situation?

[A]

Rights of Creditors:

- Secured Creditor is one who holds a mortgage, charge or lien on any of the *debtor's* property. (i.e. a creditor holding 3rd party security is *not* a secured creditor in the context of the debtor's bankruptcy and the 3rd party security can be disregarded for purposes of proof).

Choices open to Secured Creditor:

Secured creditor may

- give up his security and prove for whole debt.
- realise the security and prove for the difference
- Value the security and prove for deficiency
- Rely on his security and waive right to prove.

Preferential Creditors:

Section 33 Bankruptcy Act 1914 stipulates following rank before all other debts (but not before holders of fixed charge security in respect of the proceeds of the charged assets):

- Local Rates due within past 12 months.
- Income Tax up to 5th April before Receiving Order, with maximum of one year's assessment, the Inland Revenue having the right to select the year.
- V.A.T. for past 12 months
- P.A.Y.E. (employer's) for past 12 months.
- Wages and Salaries during 17 weeks prior to receiving order with a maximum of £800 per employee.
- Certain payments under Social Insurance Acts and Employment Protection Act.

Discharge from Bankruptcy:

Undischarged bankrupt is person who has been adjudicated bankrupt and not yet received his order of discharge.

It is an offence for him to obtain credit of £50 or more without disclosing status and to trade under assumed name. Cannot also be made a director of a company without court consent.

Bankrupt's dealings with after-acquired property are valid, if bona fide and for value, unless Trustee has already intervened (Section 47). Banker basically protected therefore at law but a duty is imposed on banker after ascertaining that customer is undischarged bankrupt.

When this occurs, banker should inform Trustee in Bankruptcy or Department of Trade of existence of account and make no payments for one month unless so authorised by Trustee or the Court.

If banker considers an account is being run for a bankrupt by a nominee, e.g. his wife, then similar action recommended. Customer should be advised of bank's action — if he claims to have been discharged, he should be asked to produce his order of discharge. If in doubt, banker can make a search at the Bankruptcy Register.

Bankrupt Payee of cheque:

An open cheque payable to person known to be undischarged bankrupt should not be paid as it may belong to Trustee and payee's title may therefore be defective. If paid to payee, customer could still be liable to trustee; therefore cheque should be returned "Payee bankrupt." Banker could, if cheque paid with knowledge that payee bankrupt, be sued by Trustee for conversion. Care needed not to damage credit of drawer of cheque.

Question 13

(a) You are notified that a receiving order has been made against your customer Meredith, whose account is overdrawn to the extent of £10,400 against security legally charged by Meredith as follows:-

- Deeds of property which you estimate are valued at £8000;
- Life Policy, nominal value £10,000 surrender value £1200.

What courses of action are open to you?

(b) In similar circumstances, you hold as security only a guarantee by Jones for £9000. What action would you take?

[B]

Deed of Arrangement:

Is a voluntary assignment of his assets by a debtor to a trustee for the benefit of his creditors generally. Deeds of Arrangement Act 1914 applies but the execution of a deed of arrangement is itself an act of bankruptcy. Thus practical steps necessary after commission of act of bankruptcy need adopting but no payments out should be permitted at all if deed relates to property of customer *generally*.

Trustee under the Deed of Arrangment can give valid discharge to bank under Section 46 protection — i.e. provided it is before date of a receiving order and without notice of presentation of petition.

Trustee can open bank account in name of debtor's estate and can collect debts and proceeds of assets realised.

Cheques should not be drawn until 3 months have elapsed unless Trustee has shortened this by written notice to all creditors. Deed must be registered within seven days with Registrar of Deeds of Arrangment.

Deed becomes void if not assented to within 21 days by majority in number and value

BANKRUPTCY

of creditors. Any dissenting creditor can present a bankruptcy petition based on the execution of Deed of Arrangement within 3 months (or lesser period if put on shorter notice by Trustee).

Question 14

You receive at your branch a letter from a well-known firm of solicitors informing you that one of their partners has been appointed trustee under a Deed of Arrangement executed by your customer Homewear Products. A certified copy of the deed is enclosed.

You are aware that the partnership, Homewear Products, has been having problems for some time but there is at present a credit balance of £1374 on the account. No security or safe custody items are held.

What action would you take and why?

[B]

Section 3

Types of Account

PRIVATE INDIVIDUAL

REFERENCES:

Traditionally, practice was always to take references or obtain introduction from existing bank customer. Obviously such a course is safest; there is case law whereby bankers were held to be negligent in not so doing e.g. *Ladbroke v. Todd* (1914). Nowadays, increasingly bankers do not insist on formal references and many banks now open accounts on strength of satisfactory means of identification possibly backed by search at one of the several credit reference bureaux to ensure no outstanding judgements, etc. Such a change in practice, is taken on purely commercial grounds; the banks adopting this practice taking the view that they will gain more in terms of competition and time saving than they may lose if occasionally they lose money through not having taken full references.

CLOSING UNSATISFACTORY ACCOUNTS:

Bankers not expected to have to operate an account which they consider is involving bank in risk or loss. If account in credit, notice required and should be adequate for customer to make other arrangements without undue risk of injuring his credit. Amount of "reasonable" notice would depend on nature of account — *Prosperity Ltd. v. Lloyds Bank Ltd.* (1923).

After expiry of notice credits should not be received and customer should return unused cheques.

If customer does not withdraw balance as requested, balance can be transferred to a branch suspense account and a branch cheque could then be posted to customer, this having advantage that customer's account has been closed in bank's books; therefore bank cannot be faced with dilemma if cheques and credits still come through due to customer trying to thwart bank.

TYPES OF ACCOUNT

Basically, if account overdrawn without arrangement, banker can demand repayment and close account without notice. This does not apply if debt specifically not repayable on demand; if borrowing is only a partial drawdown of larger facility, or if there is real danger that customer can claim banker's previous tolerance has created an implied credit limit.

Question 15

Mr. Walter Robins, whom you do not know, calls to ask you to open a current account in his name and has £300 cash with which to open the account. He wishes to take a cheque book there and then.

How would you deal with this situation and what are the issues involved?

[B]

DEATH OF CUSTOMER:

Account should be stopped; cheques returned "Drawer deceased."

If debit, advise personal representatives of liability; if credit, they alone can give effective discharge but only after Probate or Letters of Administration.

All mandates cancelled e.g. third parties who were authorised to sign on account.

Usual to let solicitors of interested parties inspect safe custody items which may contain will; if will held can be released to named executors or solicitors. Securities not released until Probate produced.

MENTAL DISORDER OF CUSTOMER:

Contracts entered into by persons of unsound mind are generally voidable if the other party aware of the fact.

If advised reliably that customer mentally incapacitated, account should be stopped.

All mandates cancelled but some discretion should be exercised so as to avoid disruption e.g. if standing order due for payment of life policy premium.

Formal procedure involves Court of Protection who may appoint Receiver; the Court Order will lay down the manner in which Receiver is to act.

Question 16

Two years ago your customer Rose Burton was admitted to a local mental hospital for treatment. Her current account then was Cr £1134. Shortly afterwards, her husband Ronald Burton who was known to you, called and at his request you transferred the balance of Rose Burton's account to a new account in his name, which he undertook to use to pay hospital costs and other expenses, including some debts outstanding in Rose's name.

Recently Rose Burton has fully recovered her health and, through her solicitors, is now suing for divorce on grounds of cruelty which she claims brought about her mental breakdown. You have now received a letter from her solicitors referring to the moneys which were formerly in Rose Burton's account. The solicitors claim that the moneys were not used by Mr. Burton for the purposes he stated when he gave his undertaking to the bank. The solicitors say that the bank had no authority to deal with the moneys in the way it did, and they seek reimbursement for their client. On looking at your balance list, you see that there is a credit balance of £1318 in Mr. Burton's private account, and a credit balance of £78 in the new account which was opened two years ago.

What is the bank's position, and what action would you take? What points would you consider before drafting a reply to the solicitors letter? Give reasons for your answer.

[A]

COMPANIES

SEPARATE LEGAL ENTITY:

Company has separate legal existence quite apart from directors and shareholders with a distinctive name; can sue and be sued in that name — *Salomon v. Salomon & Co. Ltd.* (1897).

As opposed to partnership, a company has perpetual succession, a seal to evidence its formal acts, limited liability of its members (there can be unlimited companies although rare) and winding-up proceedings to accommodate company ceasing to exist.

Companies are formed by compliance with statutory formalities under the various Companies Acts. All company law in the Companies Acts of 1948, 1967, 1976, 1980 and 1981 now consolidated into the Companies Act 1985.

MEMORANDUM AND ARTICLES OF ASSOCIATION:

These are two main documents to be filed when a company is being registered.

Memorandum of Association — sets out constitution and powers of *company*; any acts beyond these are *ultra vires* the company and void — *The Ashbury Carriage Co. v. Riche* (1875) and *Re Introductions Ltd.* (1969). Section 9 European Communities Act 1972 provides that a person dealing with a company in good faith may treat as *intra vires* the company and directors any act the directors decide upon, and good faith is presumed unless proved to the contrary. Doubtful whether this would protect banker if lending for *ultra vires* purpose since banker may well not be held to be acting in good faith if bank has seen and has copies of Memorandum and Articles showing purpose to be *ultra vires*.

Articles of Association — comprise rules and regulations regarding persons by whom and manner in which company's business is to be conducted.

Articles supplement memorandum but cannot enlarge upon it; powers of directors are determined by the Articles.

If directors go beyond their authority (but not beyond the powers of the *company*), then the act which is *ultra vires* the directors can be ratified by ordinary resolution of members or Articles can be amended retrospectively by special resolution.

Memorandum and Articles are registered with Registrar of Companies and are public documents; ignorance of their contents cannot thus be pleaded except to extent that European Communities Act may impact.

Topic of *ultra vires* now contained in Section 35 Companies Act 1985.

CERTIFICATE OF INCORPORATION:

Is issued by Registrar when necessary formalities complied with.

PRIVATE AND PUBLIC COMPANIES:

Under Companies Act 1948, a private company was one whose articles

- restricted the right to transfer its shares
- limited number of its members to fifty, and
- prohibited any invitation to public to subscribe for shares.

A public company was one not having these restrictions.

Companies Act 1980 repealed those restrictions and stated that a public company would be identified by its name, the Memorandum of a public company stating that company was a public company.

Name of public company must end with words "public limited company" or abbreviation of that (i.e. PLC or plc) or Welsh equivalent if registered in Wales.

Nominal value of company's allotted shared capital not to be less than £50,000.

The removal of the 1948 Act's restrictions on private companies, should provide private companies with growth and development prospects previously open only to public companies. "Private" company is now any company that is not a public company.

The Companies Act 1980 sets out detailed provisions relating to the issue of shares, distribution of profits and assets, duties of directors, loans or "quasi" loans to directors, insider dealing and some miscellaneous matters.

The 1980 Act retains the general prohibition on the provision by a company of financial assistance for the purchase of its own shares (Section 54 of the 1948 Act) except that a company can provide money for this purpose under an employees' share scheme. The Companies Act 1981 amended this area of company law considerably (see later).

COMPANIES' BANKING ACCOUNTS:

When opening account banker should obtain and retain copy of Memorandum and Articles of Association and, for a public company, a copy of Registrar's authority to commence business.

Memorandum will show powers, if any, to borrow and give security and banker should check that company is trading in accordance with its objects.

Articles will tell banker by whom affairs of company are to be conducted and in what manner. Operation of bank accounts not usually specifically covered and banker should obtain from company a completed mandate form appointing bank as bankers to the company and setting out signing arrangements on the account.

BORROWING POWERS:

A *trading* company has implied power to borrow; non-trading company cannot borrow unless so authorised in Memorandum.

Limit on borrowing powers of *company* may be given in Memorandum but unusual.

If directors' borrowing powers governed by the Companies Act 1948, Clause 79 Table A restricts extent to which directors may borrow to amount of issued share capital unless consent of general meeting obtained (borrowing in this context includes any securities given by company to cover debts or liabilities of itself or of third parties). If company registered pre 1st July 1948 and the 1929 Companies Act applies Clause 69 similarly restricts directors' borrowing powers but does not include security given by company.

Under 1948 Act, limit does not apply to "temporary" loans "from company's bankers" in ordinary course of business — however "temporary" not defined and in practice this exclusion is not usually relied upon.

Clause 79 of the 1948 Act (and Clause 69 of the 1929 Act) will not apply to a company whose articles expressly exclude the provision of Table A as a whole, expressly exclude provisions of Clause 79 (or Clause 69 if appropriate) or expressly state other limits on directors' borrowing powers.

LOANS TO DIRECTORS:

The Companies Act 1980 repealed Section 190 of the 1948 Act which had previously regulated loans to directors. The 1981 Act relaxed some aspects of rules in relation to directors in the 1980 Act. Now contained in Section 330 and Sections 332–338 of Companies Act 1985.

COMPANY AND BUSINESS NAMES

The Companies Act 1981 forbids use of a name which is the same as that of a registered company already in existence and prohibits names which are offensive or impute royal, state or other governmental connection.

The 1981 Act abolished the Register of Business names (previously governed by the Registration of Business Names Act 1916) but requires, where the trade name is not the name of the proprietor, the partners if a partnership, or the corporate name if a company, that the businesses display their owners' names and addresses at their business premises and on all business stationery. Now Section 349 Companies Act 1985.

FINANCIAL ASSISTANCE FOR ACQUISITION OF SHARES:

Section 54 of the 1948 Act made it unlawful for a company to give financial assistance for the purchase of its own or its holding company's shares. This prohibition applied whether the company was providing the financial assistance directly or indirectly and case law showed why bankers needed constantly to be on guard against possible infringements — *Heald v. O'Connor* (1971). *Selangor United Rubber Estates Ltd. v. Cradock* (1968). *Karak Rubber Co. Ltd. v. Barden* (1972). *Belmont Finance Corporation v. Williams Furniture Ltd* (1979).

Sections 42–44 of the 1981 Act amend the law concerning the giving of financial assistance by a company for acquisition of its own shares. Basic prohibition re-enacted and exceptions for public companies slightly extended. For private companies, financial assistance is permitted as long as prescribed procedures observed. Now contained in Sections 151–154 and Sections 155–158 of Companies Act 1985.

TYPES OF ACCOUNT

WINDING-UP OF COMPANIES:

Companies cannot be made "bankrupt" but may be "wound up" or go into "liquidation". This may be:

Compulsory winding up by Court under Section 222 of Companies Act 1948. Now Section 517 of Companies Act 1985.

Voluntary winding-up under Section 278. Voluntary winding-up may be either a *members'* Voluntary winding-up (when the directors have to file a "declaration of Solvency") or a *creditors'* Voluntary winding-up where declaration of solvency not made and creditors meet company to co-operate in realising the assets.

Classes and Priorities of creditors — the following priorities apply —

(1) Liquidator's costs, charges, expenses.

(2) Preferential Creditors under Section 319 Companies Act 1948. Now Section 614 Companies Act 1985.

(3) Secured creditors holding a floating charge.

(4) Unsecured creditors.

Secured creditors with fixed charges can satisfy their debts from proceeds of the assets so charged, and thus to extent of the value of their charges need not feature in above order of priority.

Question 17

Brunners Ltd. has had an account with you for some twenty years, when the company was first formed to take over a partnership of builders which had also banked at the branch. In the 1960s and 1970s the company's business expanded, but recently the nature of its operations has changed and it is now engaged only in running an hotel at a seaside holiday resort. The directors are Mr. Brown and Mr. Clarke.

A few months ago, Whites Ltd. was formed as a subsidiary of Brunners Ltd. and, like its parent, was incorporated under the Companies Act 1948 and adopted Table A. The company provides catering services and the account is also at your branch. A loan of £20,000 was made recently to Whites Ltd. against an unlimited guarantee of Brunners Ltd. supported by a legal mortgage over the hotel.

Overdrafts of up to £20,000 are now appearing on Brunner's account. You are an assistant manager of the branch and your newly-appointed manager speaks to you about the borrowing position generally in the light of Brunners Ltd.'s latest balance sheet figures, which are summarised below, together with the opening statement of affairs for Whites Ltd. The manager refers to the possibility that Brunners may be trading illegally and you agree that this may be so. You draw his attention to another problem facing the bank and you discuss the steps that now need to be taken to protect the bank in these circumstances.

Brunners Limited
Balance Sheet as at year end (Four months ago)

	£		£
Issued Capital	50,000	Freehold Property	160,000
Reserves	60,000	Fixtures & Fittings	34,000
Profit and Loss ª/c	48,000	Stock	36,000
Loans from Directors	34,000	Debtors	12,000
Sundry Creditors	38,000	Cash	4,000
Bank Overdraft	16,000		
	£246,000		£246,000

Whites Ltd.
Opening Statement 1st January (this year)

Issued Capital	£40,000	Fittings etc.	£10,000
		Motor Vehicles	20,000
		Cash	10,000
	£40,000		£40,000

Required:

(a) A statement of the problems facing the bank, and the reasons for them.

(b) Notes setting out possible solutions to the problems and indicating the steps the bank should take.

[B]

Question 18

A company banking at your branch has a substantial unsecured overdraft. This overdraft seemed safe until recently, when difficult trade conditions and obvious pressure from creditors led you to think that the company might not be able to survive the next few months. A visiting inspector suggests that it would be advisable to open a separate 'wages and salaries' account.

What has he in mind, how can such action benefit the bank and what conditions have to be fulfilled?

[B]

Question 19

Top Tanks Ltd. has a current account, which usually operates in credit, and a loan account, which is being reduced by transfers of £500 on the sixth day of each month. Whilst the transfers to the loan account are up to date, the current account has become overdrawn, and from time to time you have had to return cheques. As security, you hold a legal charge over the company's freehold factory premises and an unsupported guarantee for £20,000 by two directors.

Today you have received a letter from a firm of accountants countersigned by the directors, addressed to all creditors, saying that the company is insolvent and cannot continue in business. The letter gives notice of two meetings, to be held in 21 days' time, of shareholders and creditors, at which it will be proposed that the company be placed in liquidation, and that Mr. Jones of their firm will be proposed as liquidator. Today's ledger balances are: current account £423 credit; loan account £7513 debit.

TYPES OF ACCOUNT

(i) What action will you take now, and in the period before the meeting?
(ii) Assuming the resolutions are then passed, what steps will be necessary to protect the bank's position?

Give reasons for your answer.

[A]

Question 20

The Abacus Group of companies (A Ltd. the holding company, and B Ltd. and C Ltd. wholly-owned subsidiaries) have been your customers for many years and you have extended borrowing facilities ranging up to £1 million from time to time against unlimited cross guarantees from each of the three companies in the group, supported by debentures, incorporating fixed charges over property and floating charges over all the other assets. You last valued the break-up value of the three debentures at £1.9 million.

The Group have now decided to acquire all the share capital of Z Ltd. for £500,000, and, at the same time, the group will be restructured. A Ltd. will remain as the holding company, but the main company office and factory premises valued at £750,000 will be transferred into the name of B Ltd. from A Ltd., and a mortgage of £400,000 will be raised on this property from a merchant bank who have asked you to agree to their being first mortgagees. Z Ltd's property, valued at £100,000, will be transferred to B Ltd.

Trading will be conducted through C Ltd. and Z Ltd. and these companies intend to factor their book debts, which amount to approximately £130,000 and £80,000 per month respectively.

To assist with the acquisition and with continued expansion, your branch has been asked to lend £1.2 million to A Ltd. as working capital. Subject to Z Ltd. coming into the same security arrangements as the other companies in the group, you are prepared to help.

What steps will be involved in the security rearrangement, and what aspects should receive special attention, if any? Detail your answers for each company and the group generally. Give reasons for your answers.

[A]

Question 21

In a recent issue of the London Gazette, the following notice appeared under the heading shown. The company mentioned has an account at your branch:

The Companies Act 1948
Petitions for Compulsory Winding-up
In the High Court of Justice (Chancery Division)
Companies Court No . . . .
In the matter of X Ltd., and in the matter of the Companies Act 1948.

Notice is hereby given that a Petition for the winding-up of the above-named Company by the High Court of Justice was on the . . . . presented to the said Court by Y Limited, whose registed office is situated at . . . . in the County of London, a Creditor, and that the said Petition is directed to be heard before the Court Sitting at the Royal Courts of Justice, Strand, London, on the . . . . and any Creditor or Contributory of the said Company who is desirous to support or oppose the making of an Order on the said Petition may appear at the time of hearing, in person or by his Counsel, for that purpose, and a copy of the Petition will be furnished by the undersigned to any Creditor or Contributory of the said Company requiring such copy, on payment of the regulated charge for the same.

Z & Co., Bank Chambers, London, W.C.1. Solicitors of the Petitioners.

(i) Give a full explanation of the meaning of this, stating how it affects the company and its directors, and what course of action is required by the bank.

(ii) On the day following publication of the Notice three cheques are presented for payment on the company's account:

   (i) £270 in favour of M. Cash Ltd.
   (ii) £690 wages.
   (iii) £421 Metropolitan Water Board.

How would you deal with these cheques and why?

[B]

PARTNERSHIPS

DEFINITION:
SECTION 1 PARTNERSHIP ACT 1890 —

"Relation which subsists between persons carrying on a business in common with a view to profit."

Not a separate legal entity as is a company.

FORMATION:

By agreement; can be oral, written (Articles of Partnership), by deed (Deed of Partnership).

Unless expressly varied by the partners, the provisions of Partnership Act apply.

PARTNERS' AUTHORITY:

Every general partner is agent of firm and of other partners for business of partnership; all acts thus bind all partners and firm if within usual course of business and unless other party knew partner concerned had no authority or did not know or believe him to be a partner.

IMPLIED POWERS:

To sell and buy goods for business
To give valid discharge to debtors
To hire servants for firm's business
To draw cheques (unless not in usual course of business)

Additionally partner in a *trading* firm can bind firm:

TYPES OF ACCOUNT

By drawing, accepting, endorsing bills of exchange etc. in name of firm
By borrowing money on credit of firm
By pledging partnership assets for purposes of firm's business.

Partner exceeding authority is personally liable. If Articles or Deed restricts a partner's powers, firm still liable to outside parties unaware of restriction.

LIABILITY FOR DEBTS OF FIRM:

Under the Act all partners are jointly liable for debts incurred whilst partners. Although liability joint, Act makes each partner (and his estate) fully liable for any deficiency after realisation of firm's assets, subject to prior payment of private creditors. When lending to partnerships, personal guarantees not required as partners already personally liable.

DISSOLUTION:

Can be dissolved by:

- expiry of agreed fixed term
- fulfillment of specific objective for which partnership formed
- by any partner giving notice or by mutual consent
- by death or bankruptcy of partner
- by partner allowing his share of partnership property to be charged under option of other partners
- if it becomes unlawful.

Court has power to dissolve:

- if partner is mentally incapable under Court of Protection
- where partner permanently incapable of acting as partner
- where partner has been guilty of conduct prejudicial to firm's business
- where partner persistently breaks partnership agreement
- where business can only be continued at a loss
- where Court considers it to be just and equitable.

Assets would be applied in following order of priority:

In paying debts to third persons.
In repaying any loans made by partners.
In repaying capital put in by partners.
Residue (if any) to partners in profit sharing ratio.

OPENING PARTNERSHIP ACCOUNT:

Banker not obliged to see Articles or Deed of Partnership — if he does, he is bound by contents.

Mandate giving signing instructions etc. should be signed by all partners and should make them jointly and severally liable.

Any one partner can stop a cheque whether he signed it or not.

As death or bankruptcy of partner dissolves firm, all mandates must thereupon be treated as cancelled.

LENDING TO PARTNERSHIPS:

Although any partner has implied power to borrow, banker obtains undertaking signed by all partners to be liable for any overdrafts — this usually incorporated in bank mandate.

With non-trading firms there is no implied power to overdraw, therefore the express power contained in mandate is essential.

DEATH OF A PARTNER:

Partnership dissolved; surviving partners' duty to wind up its affairs. They can continue banking account for this purpose; fresh mandate needed from all surviving partners unless all sign.

If account debit — should be broken if it is necessary to prevent operation of Clayton's Case, as, deceased estate not liable for debts incurred after date of death. Surviving partners can operate new account for purposes of winding up and can pledge partnership property if borrowing needed — In *Re Bourne* (1906).

If surviving partners are to continue the business this will constitute fresh partnership and will entail fresh documentation for bank.

Cheques signed by deceased partner presented after death could be paid from practical viewpoint; surviving partners should ideally confirm the payments.

BANKRUPTCY OF PARTNER:

Cheques drawn by partner before his bankruptcy should ideally be confirmed by solvent partners; any cheques dated afterwards *must* be.

Assuming usual joint and several liability obtains, account must be broken — procedure similar to that upon death.

MENTAL DISORDER OF PARTNER:

Firm not automatically dissolved unless Articles or Deed of Partnership say so. Application may be made to the Court for dissolution by another partner, or on behalf of mentally disabled partner.

If account debit, safest course is to break the account.

If account credit, fresh mandate should be obtained.

RETIREMENT OF PARTNER:

If remaining partners continue, they are technically creating a fresh partnership and new forms should be signed.

BANKRUPTCY OF PARTNERSHIP:

This involves bankruptcy of every partner in the firm and the firm's and partners' private accounts must be stopped.

Partnership property will be applied in payment of debts of firm, and separate property of each partner applied separately in payment of their separate debts. Surplus, if any, on joint estate (i.e. proceeds of partnership property) would go towards payment of separate estates and vice versa.

TYPES OF ACCOUNT

JOINT ACCOUNTS

Important to distinguish from partnership accounts since different effect in event of bankruptcy or mental disorder as regards discharge to bank.

Mandate — signed by all parties stating how and by whom account to be operated. Should contain express authority to bank to permit overdraft at request of each signatory as otherwise all the parties will not be even jointly liable unless all sign the cheques. Mandate will incorporate joint and several liability.

If authority to be given to outside party to sign on the account, all parties to account must sign the authority. Where one party signs alone, a cheque drawn by one party may be altered by another, and either (or any) party can stop payment of a cheque irrespective of whether or not they signed it.

DEATH OF PARTY TO ACCOUNT:

If account credit, balance may be drawn by survivors and banker not concerned with claim of deceased's representatives; they must resolve position with surviving parties.

If account debit, bank should break account to avoid Clayton's Case if banker is looking to the deceased party's estate for repayment and providing joint and several liability exists.

Whether debit or credit, any cheques not signed by all survivors should not be paid strictly speaking; but if account credit this is usually done.

If securities are held in joint names, a discharge from the survivor(s) and the deceased's personal representatives would be needed as bank may not know whether items held were owned jointly or in common; however the usual bank mandate specifically covers this point by stating that all securities (as well as the balance of the account) are to be held to the order of the survivor(s).

BANKRUPTCY OF PARTY TO JOINT ACCOUNT:

Mandate is cancelled and balance has to be apportioned between solvent party and Trustee in Bankruptcy; bank not concerned with apportionment but requires discharge of solvent party and Trustee.

Even if account in credit, it has to be stopped.

If debit, must be stopped to enable banker (if joint and several liability obtained) to prove on bankrupt's estate without prejudicing his rights against the other party.

MENTAL DISORDER OF PARTY TO JOINT ACCOUNT:

Account should be stopped as in case of partnership account, pending instructions from the other parties and the Receiver appointed by the Court of Protection.

Question 22

Leslie and Joan Charles have a joint account at your branch, operating under the bank's usual mandate form, incorporating joint and several liability, and authorising cheques to be paid on the signature of either of them. Recently Joan Charles drew a cheque for £1440 in favour of a local furrier, but before it was presented you received a visit from Leslie Charles who countermanded payment.

He said that he was not going to allow his wife to buy a fur coat out of his earnings when other items were needed for the family. You duly returned the cheque with the answer "Payment countermanded" when it was presented three days ago.

Today, Joan Charles calls to see you, in some distress. She says that there are disagreements over money, but that the funds in the account have all been provided by her and the cheque must be paid on re-presentation. The balance on the account is £2103 credit.

How would you deal with this situation?

Give reasons for your answer.

[B]

Question 23

State briefly giving reasons, what steps you would take, as a banker, with regard to a credit account if you received notice of (a) the death of, and (b) the making of a Receiving Order against (i) a party to a joint account, (ii) a partner in a partnership account.

Would your action differ if in each instance the account was overdrawn?

[B]

Question 24

Mr. Gilbert and Mr. Ruddle are in partnership and their account is overdrawn £1350 against an unsecured limit £1500. The account was opened some years ago at the request of Mr. Gilbert who was known to the bank as a man of some means, and it has been used for a small business which Mr. Gilbert largely financed, leaving the daily running to Mr. Ruddle. The usual bank mandate was taken allowing either to sign. Mr. Ruddle calls to tell you of the death of Mr. Gilbert and brings the death certificate for your inspection. He asks to continue the account on the existing basis in his sole name, deleting the name of Mr. Gilbert and retaining the existing limit. The bank is aware that Mr. Gilbert's estate will probably realise £100,000 and that there are shares in safe custody worth £20,000.

How should the branch deal with this request?

[A]

Question 25

(a) Smith, Hall and Green trade as Central T.V. and Video Company, and the bank's mandate authorises any one of the partners to sign on behalf of the firm. Hall and Green have written to you requesting that from receipt of their letter, no further cheques on the account signed by Smith alone are to be paid without reference to the other two partners. They request that the outstanding balance, except for £600, be transferred into a new account in their joint names. The £600 on the "old" account is to meet cheques that have been issued but not presented.

State how you would deal with this request.

(b) You have a partnership account at your branch for Jones and Green and the mandate for signing the cheques states that all cheques for more than £200 must be signed by both partners.

Jones has now called to see you and states that several cheques, each for £200 or more, totalling £1,450, have been signed by Green alone, and have been passed by the bank for payment.

What is the bank's position regarding this matter?

[B]

Section 4
Executors and Administrators

Executor:
person appointed in will by testator and to whom Probate is granted — duty is to pay deceased's debts and distribute assets as instructed in will.

Probate:
the official copy of will with certificate showing it has been proved.

Administrator:
person appointed by Court to administer estate of the deceased when no will left. Is granted Letters of Administration and distributes estate according to the law of intestacy.

Executors and Administrators are called the deceased's "legal personal representatives."

Letters of Administration with the will annexed
— are granted when the deceased left a will but did not name an executor. The administrator then carries out the terms of the will as would an executor.

Releasing the will:
when banker holds the will, he should release this only after evidence of death against the receipt or on instructions of the named executor(s). When names not initially known, the packet containing will should be opened in presence of interested parties and/or their solicitor to ascertain who is executor.

Title of executor and administrator not complete until will proved or letters of administration granted respectively.

Banker therefore cannot let personal representatives deal with assets of deceased until Probate or Letters of Administration granted, but a schedule of securities and other items held will be required to enable probate to be obtained.

Opening an Account:
if sole executor or administrator then only the person himself can sign on the account.

If more than one executor or administrator, one of them can act for the rest (unlike joint accounts) legally; however in practice banker would take mandate signed by all setting out clearly how and by whom account to be operated.

Normal practice is to open account as follows:

"X, Y and Z."
"Executors of A deceased."

Advances to Personal Representatives:
a facility is usually called for to enable Capital Transfer Tax to be paid so that Probate (or Letters of Administration if no will) can be obtained.

Legally, executors have power to pledge assets of the estate before probate (but not administrators) but this is not of practical significance to the lending banker since the pledge is valid only when probate granted.

Usual bank mandate will make executors (or adminstrators) jointly and severally liable and contain an undertaking to repay advance out of first proceeds of realisation of estate. The solicitors acting for the executors (or administrators) would also normally be asked to undertake to apply for probate (or letters of administration) in favour of the parties applying for the advance.

Question 26

The three executors named in the will of a deceased customer wish to open an Executor's account on which they require to borrow £27,650 to pay the Capital Transfer Tax and expenses to enable them to obtain Grant of Probate of the will.

Detail the steps which should be taken to satisfy their requests giving full reasons for any steps which you advocate. Would the procedure differ if the customer had died intestate and a similar request was made by the widow, as next of kin, who proposed to take out Letters of Administration?

[B]

TRUSTEES

Trustee:
a person to whom some sort of estate is conveyed, devised, bequeathed in trust for another. Need not arise out of some person's death and can arise by implication where one person, in a fiduciary capacity, holds property belonging to another.

Duties are different from those of executor as a trustee has the legal possession and ownership of the property intended for the benefit of other persons, often with full powers of management over it.

Trustee's Powers:
are conferred upon him by the settlement or will creating the trust and/or by statute — Trustee Act 1925.

Opening an Account:
banker should see the document creating the trust; unless it states otherwise, all trustees have to sign. Bank mandate cannot override terms of trust deed.

Open account in names of trustees followed by "Trustees of . . . ."

Lending to Trustees:
Trustees will be personally liable and bank mandate will make them jointly and severally so.

EXECUTORS AND ADMINISTRATORS

If security offered, i.e. trust security, the banker must check that the borrowing and the giving of the security are authorised by the terms of the trust.

Death of Trustee:
on death of one of two or more trustees, survivors may continue to act unless trust deed calls for appointment of new trustee.

On death of sole trustee, his personal representatives may act as trustee pending appointment, by them or as directed by trust deed, of a new trustee.

Bankruptcy of Trustee:
does not determine right to act unless trust deed provides otherwise. An application could be made to Court for a new trustee to be appointed; Section 41 of Trustee Act 1925 enables court to appoint trustee(s) wherever difficulties are experienced in trying to appoint new trustees without the court's assistance.

Mental Disorder:
further operations on a trust account should not be permitted by a trustee who is mentally incapacitated.

Question 27

Your customer, Miss Ann Burns, aged 22, is reversioner to the estate of her late father upon the death of her mother, who has a life interest. The mother and the deceased's brother are trustees of the estate, which consists of properties worth some £200,000.

Miss Brown wishes to raise £17,500 to purchase a car and furnish her rented flat and her uncle has suggested to you that the trustees should borrow the amount in their joint names, mortgaging to the bank as security some freehold deeds, part of the estate she will ultimately inherit; alternatively, that she herself should borrow and give a charge over her interest in the property in question. Upon reaching the age of 25 she will become entitled to a legacy of £25,000 under the grandfather's will and, in the meantime should have no difficulty in meeting interest out of her personal earned income.

Set out briefly the principal technical considerations which arise with each of the securities offered and say in which manner you would prefer to handle the proposition. You may assume that the advance is desirable in view of the standing of the family and its long association with your bank.

[A]

Question 28

Your customer T. Talbot died last week. You receive a visit from a young man who tells you that he is P. Talbot your late customer's son: he produces his father's will in which he is named as executor and asks that a collection of gold coins which his father left with you in safe custody be given up to him so that he can take it away for probate valuation.

What reply would you give?

[B]

Question 29

John Horne, a retired man, has maintained small accounts with your branch for many years. Today, with credit balances of £52 on the current account and £296 on the deposit accounts in his name, you receive a visit from Mrs. Horne, who tells you that her husband died ten days ago in hospital.

She says she knows he has not left a will and, as his estate is very small, she has been advised that she need not take out letters of administration. She asks you to transfer the balances in her deceased husband's name to her account, which you ascertain is maintained at a local branch of your bank.

How would you proceed? Give reasons for your answer.

[B]

Question 30

Mr. R. Bandim immigrated to the U.K. some 20 years ago and started to earn his living by running a stall on a market where he sold cloth. In 1978 he rented a shop in the street from which his stall still operated, and there his wife ran a delicatessen business on his behalf. The local branch of a clearing bank opened an account for Mr. Bandim to handle the delicatessen business and, as far as the bank knew, Mr. Bandim had no other account. In 1981, Mr. Bandim asked for a five year loan of £5000 to go towards the purchase of a flat costing £30,000; with him finding the balance of £25,000 in cash. The bank agreed to this and the advance, which was serviced satisfactorily, was secured by a legal mortgage over the flat property which was registered in the name of Mr. Bandim.

Recently a man telephoned to say that he was Mr. Bandim's brother, and that Mr. Bandim had died following a heart attack. He further said that Mrs. Bandim was the common-law wife of Mr. Bandim and no doubt the bank would take note of that in its dealings with Mr. Bandim's affairs. Moreover, Mr. Bandim had at least two more businesses which he knew about. He gave his name and address.

Within an hour, Mrs. Bandim called at the bank and, as soon as the manager had expressed his sympathy, she said that she would be continuing the business of the shop, that she had the previous day's takings to pay in, and that she required the will which she understood to be in safe custody. She was aware of the other businesses but had no knowledge of them.

The branch had taken the precaution of seeing if they held a will before Mrs. Bandim called and the manager had to tell her that there was no will in their possession, at which Mrs. Bandim became distraught, saying that her husband had promised her that there was a will in her favour held at the bank. She admitted that she was not married to Mr. Bandim, with whom she had been living for 5 years. She now regarded the delicatessen as her own and requested the account to be transferred into her name. The balance of Mr. Bandim's accounts are Current Account — £800 Credit, Loan Account £4300 Debit.

How do you think the manager should handle this situation?

[A]

Section 5

The Paying and Collecting Banker

THE PAYING BANKER:

Practical dangers are that a cheque has been paid that has been:
- Stopped
- Post-dated
- Forged
- Fraudulently altered

Also banker may have paid a cheque to a person not entitled to it or for an unlawful purpose.

Stopped Cheques:
Customer's right to countermand payment exists up to time of *payment*; even if banker has told holder that cheque will be paid on presentation.

Stop payment instructions must actually come to notice of banker — *Curtice v. London City and Midland Bank Ltd.* (1908). Branches of a bank treated as being independent for purposes of stop payments.

Drawer must furnish accurate description of cheque — *Westminster Bank v. Hilton* (1926).

Banker who pays stopped cheques may face two-fold action:

- For paying stopped cheque
- For wrongfully dishonouring other cheques due to balance having wrongly been depleted due to payment of "stop."

Banker has no right of subrogation but can claim goods, if any and if identifiable in respect of which cheque issued.

Post-dated cheques:
not invalid but can involve banker in loss. If cheque paid before due date:

- Customer may die or become bankrupt
- Customer may stop payment
- Other cheques may wrongly be dishonoured.

Drawer's Signature Forged:
- If doubt over signature care needed not to damage customer's credit. If necessary to return answer could be "Drawer's signature requires confirmation."
- If banker pays cheque with forged signature, he cannot debit customer's account since he has no mandate, unless:
  - customer knows of forgery and unreasonably delays advising bank;
  - customer has induced bank to rely on the forgery.

Safeguards against forgery:
- Care in handing out for first time cheque books to new customers. (Take satisfactory references or check identity)
- Care to be exercised when sending out cheque books; ideally send only against properly-signed orders, or hand direct to customer or known agent.
- Note carefully any cheques stolen and stop payment where possible.
- Special care needed if cheque not drawn on standard form e.g. as with "club" cheques.

Facsimile Signatures:
With cheques bearing these, the banker cannot know if the "signature" was placed on the cheque under proper authority. Bank therefore should take indemnity from customer covering any loss banker could otherwise incur.

Fraudulent alteration of amount:
Fraudulently raising the amount is a material alteration and banker has no mandate to debit customer's account. Customer owes duty to banker to exercise reasonable care, otherwise customer bears any loss — *London Joint Stock Bank v. MacMillan and Arthur* (1918).

Banker stands loss if alteration is apparent, or if non-apparent but customer exercised proper care.

Drawer stands loss if he fails to exercise care and alteration non-apparent.

Payee's Name fraudulently altered:
No duty owed by customer to draw lines and leave no spaces before and after payee's name — *Slingsby v. District Bank* (1932).

Payment to wrong person or for unlawful purpose:
Banker may be liable if he pays cheque, even if correctly drawn within mandate, if he knows or ought to know it has been drawn for illegal purpose. In *Selangor United Rubber Estates Ltd. v. Cradock* (1968) cheque paid was in connection with the purchase by a company of its own shares and bank was liable for failing to exercise reasonable care and skill in paying the cheque.

Forged or unauthorised endorsements:
Under Section 59 Bills of Exchange Act 1882 banker gets good discharge by payment to *holder* if in good faith and without notice of defective title.

Person claiming under forged or unauthorised endorsement is *not* a holder and banker will get no discharge, and will be liable to true owner for conversion.

Practical difficulty of paying banker recognised by Section 60 which protects banker should endorsement on cheque be forged, provided it is paid in good faith, in ordinary course of business and endorsement purports to be in order.

Banker does not pay in ordinary course of business if he pays outside business hours

THE PAYING AND COLLECTING BANKER

— but *Baines v. National Provincial Bank Ltd* (1927) held that bank entitled to reasonable margin after closing time to deal with customers on premises.

Banker does not pay in ordinary course of business if he pays crossed cheque contrary to the crossing. Section 80 protects banker paying a crossed cheque if paid in good faith, without negligence and to a banker in accordance with the crossing.

THE COLLECTING BANKER:

Banker when collecting cheques for customer may be liable in an action for conversion; he can claim to be indemnified by his customer and debit customer with amount banker has to pay to true owner.

As customer would usually be involved in actions for conversion, this right of indemnity is usual of little practical value.

Main statutory protection — Sections 4 & 5 Cheques Act 1957 — is that where banker, in good faith and without negligence, receives payment for a customer or, having credited a customer's account, receives payment for himself, and customer has no title or defective title, banker does not incur any liability to true owner by reason only of having received payment for it.

Danger to collecting banker is that his statutory protection may be lost if he is held to be negligent.

Negligence not defined by the Act but it has been held that "the test of negligence is whether the transaction of paying in a given cheque, coupled with the circumstances antecedent and present, were so out of the ordinary course that it ought to have aroused doubts in the banker's mind and caused him to make enquiry."

Case Law has to be guide to what can constitute negligence, in the absence of a statutory definition.

Following cases have been held to constitute negligence:

- Failure to take up references when opening an account; *Ladbroke v. Todd* (1914) or to ensure that they are genuine; *Guardians of St. John's, Hampstead v. Barclays Bank Ltd.* (1923), and *Lumsden & Co. v. London Trustee Savings Bank* (1971). This last case is interesting because the plaintiffs' damages were reduced by 10% because of their contributory negligence in the way in which they drew their cheques.
- Collecting a cheque crossed "Account Payee" for a person other than the specified payee — even if payable to a specified payee "or bearer": *House Property Company of London v. London County and Westminster Bank* (1915). Omission to see that the endorsement is in order: *Bavins, Jnr. and Sims v. London and South Western Bank* (1900): *Turner v. London and Provincial Bank* (1903): *Slingsby v. District Bank Ltd.* (1931).
- Collecting *without enquiry* cheques payable to the *collecting bank* for the account of an employee of the drawer: *Lloyds Bank Ltd. v. Chartered Bank of India, Australia and China* (1929).
- Collecting *without enquiry* a cheque for the personal account of an agent, the cheque being payable to such agent and drawn *by him* on behalf of his principal: *Midland Bank Ltd. v. Reckitt* (1933).
- Collecting *without enquiry* a cheque in favour of one Company for the account of

another Company: *London and Montrose Shipbuilding Company v. Barclays Bank Ltd.* (1926).
- Collecting, without enquiry, for the private account of an official of a company a cheque payable to the company and endorsed by that official. This was held to be negligence in the case of *Underwood v. Bank of Liverpool* (1924) even though the official was the *sole* director of a "one man company".
- Similarly, collecting a cheque payable to a firm for the private account of one partner without making enquiry.
- Collecting for his private account cheques payable to an official (e.g. Collector of Rates) in his official capacity, without special authority: similarly, collecting for the private account of an agent a warrant payable to him in his capacity of agent. viz.: "D. McGaw for Marquess of Bute": *Bute v. Barclays Bank Ltd.* (1954).
- Collecting *without enquiry* cheques drawn by a Company or Firm in favour of *third parties* and paid in for the credit of an employee of the drawer or for credit of the wife of such an employee — *Lloyds Bank Ltd. v. EB Savory & Co* (1932).

In the Savory Case, cheques payable to bearer drawn by a firm were collected without enquiry, some for an employee of the firm, some for an employee's wife. The cheques were paid in at one branch for credit of an account at another branch, which latter branch was ignorant of the connection between their customer and the drawer of the cheques. It was held that this was negligence and that knowledge of the customer's standing is knowledge by the **bank**, not by any particular branch.

Some cases in which banks succeeded in retaining their protection by showing they made satisfactory enquiries and received satisfactory replies are:
- *Smith and Baldwin v. Barclays Bank Ltd.* (1944)
- *Slingsby v. Westminster Bank Ltd.* (1930)
- *Renmount Estates Ltd. v. National Provincial Bank Ltd.* (1945)
- *Marfani & Co. Ltd. v. Midland Bank Ltd.* (1968).

If a banker exchanges a cheque, the banker is collecting for itself and not for a customer and is not therefore protected by Section 4 as a collecting banker. Further, the bank obtains no protection if the cheque is tainted with forgery, and if the cheque is crossed "Not Negotiable" — even though the endorsements are genuine — the bank's title will be defeated if the title of the transferor is defective (e.g. the cheque could have been stolen after endorsement).

Crossed Cheques:
Object of crossing a cheque is to prevent its being presented by a person for whom it is not intended.

Crossings cannot guarantee this but will make it more difficult for a thief to cash cheques for crossed cheques must be paid to a banker.

"Not Negotiable" Crossings:
The words "Not Negotiable" as part of the crossing of a cheque prevent the person who takes it from having or being able to give a better title to it than that of the person from whom he took it" — Section 81 Bills of Exchange Act 1882.

Transferability of cheque not prevented, and if person who transfers it has good title, the transferee will have good title and the cheque may continue to change hands. If crossed cheque marked "Not Negotiable" has been passed from hand to hand and there is no defect of title, the holder can recover the amount of the cheque and, if the banker refuses to pay the cheque, the holder can sue the drawer.

THE PAYING AND COLLECTING BANKER

If crossed "Not Negotiable" and there is a defect of title the real holder for value can claim the amount from the last holder who innocently receives payment of it through his bank. The last holder must recover from his immediate transferor.

"Account Payee only" Crossings:
No statutory significance.

Nevertheless, such crossing significant to collecting banker since it has been held negligent to collect a cheque so marked for anyone other than the specified payee.

Banker may not lose protection if he makes enquiries and receives satisfactory answers to them — *Bevan v. National Bank Ltd.* (1906).

Question 31

Discuss the position of a banker who

(a) Pays (i) a post dated cheque;
          (ii) a cheque of which payment has been countermanded;
          (iii) a cheque bearing a forged endorsement.

(b) Collects (i) an uncrossed cheque;
             (ii) a crossed cheque.

(c) Exchanges a cheque crossed "Not negotiable".

[B]

Question 32

Your customer Jack agrees to sell a car to another customer, Hank for £2000. To give time for trying the car, Hank issues an open cheque at five minutes before closing time, knowing that Jack cannot reach the bank before closing time. Jack, however, goes to a nearby sub-branch, pays the cheque in for the credit of his account at the main branch, and asks to be told whether the cheque is paid. On reaching the main office thirty minutes after closing time the sub-branch clerk has the cheque paid and telephones Jack accordingly. The next morning Hank wants to stop payment, and subsequently his lawyers claim restitution on grounds that by paying the cheque after closing time the bank has acted in breach of its obligations to Hank as a customer. They also contend that the cheque had not been paid in the ordinary course of business.

Discuss the bank's position and say how the lawyers' letter should be dealt with.

[B]

Question 33

Ann Price, a well-known journalist on a national newspaper, calls to see you and informs you that she has recently married Roger Shepherd, another journalist. She says, however, that she will wish to continue to write her books and articles under the name by which she is well known, and she tenders for collection for her account three cheques: one for £340 in favour of Ann Price, one for £89 in favour of Ann Shepherd, and one for £4180 in favour of Roger Shepherd, endorsed by him.

What action would you take? Give reasons for your answer.

[B]

Question 34

Venners Ltd., market gardeners, operate a current account in substantial credit, and the two directors keep good balances on their own current and deposit accounts. You recently joined the branch and have noticed that the company regularly pays into its account unendorsed cheques in favour of Venners (Seeds) Ltd. and on making enquiries you are told that Venners (Seeds) Ltd. is a wholly-owned subsidiary of Venners Ltd. but it does not have an account in its own name at your bank.

How would you recommend that this situation be dealt with? Give reasons for your answer.

[A]

Question 35

Guy James maintains at your branch an account designated The Bollin Printing Company, the name under which he trades. He paid into the account a crossed cheque for £1,000 payable to The Bollin Printing Company or order. He did not endorse the cheque and was allowed to draw against it immediately. Three days later the cheque was returned unpaid with the answer "Orders not to pay".

Has the bank any claim against the drawer and, if so, what?

[B]

Question 36

Redline Ltd. drew a cheque for £700 payable to Hill and posted it to him. It was received at his office and stolen by Gay who persuaded a branch shop of your valuable customer, Big Value Ltd., to cash it for him. Big Value's manager paid it in for the company's account at one of your bank's branches. As the cheque was crossed "account payee only" the branch raised queries but received answers from the shop manager which satisfied them as to the bona fides of the transaction. Later you receive a demand from a solicitor for the payment of the whole sum to his client, Hill.

Discuss your position as a banker, saying how the situation should be dealt with and what protection, if any, is given by the Bills of Exchange Act 1882, and the Cheques Act 1957.

[B]

Section 6
Security for Advances

Characteristics of good security:
- Simplicity of title
- Stability of value
- Adequate margin for loss
- Absence of liability
- Cheapness and ease of transfer
- Readiness of realisability.

"Direct" Security:
Is security provided by borrower to secure own account.

"Third Party" Security:
Is security provided by a third party to secure the customer's liabilities.

(Nowadays all third party security invites banker to consider carefully whether person providing security should receive independent legal advice.)

TYPES OF SECURITY:

STOCK EXCHANGE SECURITIES:

Registered Securities (i.e. ownership evidenced by certificate issued in name of owner, the company keeping a register of stocks and shares).

Legal transfer evidenced by certificate together with signed transfer being sent to Registrar of company who amends register and issues certificate in new owner's name.

Bank can take either equitable or legal title.

Equitable Charge over shares:
Mere deposit of shares will give banker equitable title but Memorandum of Deposit should be taken to establish clearly terms under which shares held. Additionally, a

signed transfer form is usually taken so that banker could effect sale without going to court.

Transferee would usually be the bank's nominee company, but often transferee and date not inserted at outset (referred to as a "blank transfer.")

Some banks do not take blank transfers; some take blank transfers as their normal practice but dispense with them in certain cases.

Legal Charge over shares:
Charge taken by memorandum of deposit but shares are actually transferred, at the time into name of bank (or more usually its nominee company). Certificate thus held with bank as registered owner.

Forged Transfers:
In *Lord Mayor of Sheffield v. Barclay* (1905) it was held that banker who sends in for registration a forged transfer indemnifies the company which can act on assumption transfer genuine.

Legal and Equitable Charges compared:
Legal Charge:

Advantages

- Bank's legal title prior to all equitable charges of which it had no notice when taking security.
- Banker as registered owner can sell at any time on own signature.

Disadvantages

- Banker may be liable if shares partly paid for any unpaid calls; if transfer forged bank may lose its security.
- Security more costly and complicated.

Equitable Charge:

Advantages

- Relatively simple to take
- Banker avoids liability on shares.

Disadvantages

- Bank may lose security by forfeiture for non-payment of calls.
- Is subordinated to prior equitable title
- All communications re shares continue to go direct to customer.

Bearer Securities:
Title passes by delivery and mere deposit of bond or certificate will give bank a valid legal title if taken for value, in good faith and without notice of defect of title in depositor.

Memorandum of Deposit preferable as evidence of terms of deposit.

Bearer securities being fully negotiable become security by way of pledge.

Partly Paid Shares:
Banker if registered holder becomes liable for all calls.

If banker not registered holder and calls are made, banker may have to lend more to enable calls to be met to avoid his security being forfeited.

Partly paid shares not so marketable.

NATIONAL SAVINGS SECURITIES (E.G. NATIONAL SAVINGS CERTIFICATES, PREMIUM SAVINGS BONDS)

These are not very good banking security as charges over them cannot be protected by registration and owner can sell them or obtain new certificate or bond without bank's knowledge.

Where honesty of customer beyond doubt banker may take deposit of certificates or bonds with signed repayment form authorising remittance direct to bank.

Unquoted Shares:
Shares not dealt with on Stock Exchange are difficult to dispose of but can be very valuable.

Shares difficult to value as security due to absence of market price.

Question 37

(a) Mrs. King, who has kept a modest account with North Bank for some years, obtains borrowing facilities of £3000 to assist in redecoration and refurnishing of her house and gives the bank as security an equitable charge by way of a memorandum of deposit over various shares registered in her name. She fails to repay in accordance with the arrangement; the bank makes formal demand for the repayment of the debt and seeks to enforce its security. It then emerges that the shares were held by her as trustee for her children. What is the bank's position?

(b) A customer lodges with your branch as security for his borrowing various share certificates, some of which are partly paid. Your manager tells you to go ahead with arrangements to transfer all but the partly paid shares into the name of the bank's nominee company, but tells you that the partly paid shares should be held under an equitable mortgage only. What are the reasons for this differentiation?

[B]

Question 38

A customer who died recently left an overdraft against which the following security is held:-

(i) £400 4% Victory Bonds (Bearer).

(ii) 100 Shares International Nickel Co. of Canada Common Stock (in "marking name" and endorsed).

(iii) 100 Shares International Nickel Co. of Canada Common Stock (in own name and endorsed).

(iv) 2,000 Ordinary £1 Shares Southtown Regal Cinema Ltd. — local public company. (In own name: fully executed and stamped transfers to Bank's Nominee Company held unregistered: notice of charge given to Cinema Company who declined to accept).

(v) £100 Southtown Corporation 5½% Stock 1986–90. (In own name: no transfers held and no notice given to Registrar).

All items were left with the bank for safe keeping many years ago by the customer and the bank's standard memorandum of deposit was signed subsequently when overdraft facilities were first granted.

You are now informed that these securities were originally the property of the customer's wife who died leaving all her estate to her brother subject to the life interest of her husband, who was appointed sole executor and obtained probate of her Will. The brother now demands the securities from the bank and insists that any interest or dividends received after the date of death shall be remitted to him. What is the bank's position?

[B]

Question 39

Mr. Parker has a current account and a loan account at your Country Branch, and there is also a joint current account maintained in his name and that of his wife. This last account operates under a joint and several mandate, with either to sign. Country Branch has agreed borrowing facilities of £3000 on Mr. Parker's loan account and this is being reduced at £150 per month. Repayments are up to date. Occasionally, small borrowing facilities have been allowed on the joint account without prior arrangement.

As security, the bank holds one thousand shares in Fortune Ltd., lodged by Mr. Parker on a memorandum of deposit, securing all his liabilities to the bank.

The balances on the accounts are:

Mr. Parker Current a/c — Credit £321
Mr. Parker Loan a/c — Debit £1900
Mr. & Mrs. Parker Current a/c — Debit £310

You are the manager of Country Branch, and during your absence on holiday, the bank notices in the financial press that dealings in the shares of Fortune Ltd. have been suspended. A worried assistant manager writes to Mr. Parker mentioning this and saying that he has consequently stopped all the accounts, after transferring Mr. Parker's credit balance in reduction of the joint account. The same day he dishonours a cheque for £140 drawn by Mr. Parker on his current account with the answer "Refer to Drawer".

You return to the office on the day following these events and, when perusing the files, you notice the action that has been taken.

What action would you take, and what advice would you give your assistant manager? Give reasons for your answer.

[A]

DEBENTURES:

Debenture is document given by company as evidence of loan and any charge securing it.

Companies can make public issues of debenture stock but in banking context, the banker is mainly concerned with debentures executed by companies in favour of bank as security for bank finance.

Debenture offered by newly-formed company:
— danger of fraudulent conveyance — In *re Simms* (1930).

SECURITY FOR ADVANCES

Bank form of Debenture:
Usually an all-monies charge incorporating fixed and floating charges.

Fixed charge usually given on freehold property and other permanent assets with view to preventing company from disposing of these.

Fixed Charge nowadays usually taken also over book debts (i.e. company's debtors) to give bank priority over preferential creditors.

Floating Charge:
- charge given on assets of a company in such form that company may deal with those assets in the ordinary course of its business.
- characteristics of floating charge explained in *Re Yorkshire Woolcombers' Association* (1903).
- floating charge created within 12 months of commencement of winding up, unless it is proved that company was solvent when charge given, will be invalid except for "fresh" borrowing — i.e. borrowing permitted on or subsequent to creation of charge — Section 322 Companies Act 1948 (Now Section 615 Companies Act 1985). Rule in Clayton's Case will work in favour of bank with a running account — *Re Thomas Mortimer Ltd.* (1925) and *Re Yeovil Glove Co. Ltd.* (1965).
- floating charge ranks behind preferential creditors under Section 319 Companies Act 1948 (Now Section 614 Companies Act 1985).

Disadvantages of Floating Charge:

- It is only an equitable charge;
- It does not prevent the company from making specific charges unless otherwise agreed;
- The holder of a floating charge may lose his priority if specific mortgages are made without notice of such agreement;
- It does not cover previous advances if the company is wound up within twelve months of the creation of the charge unless it is proved that the company was solvent at the time of creating the charge;
- The charge "remains dormant" or "floats" whilst the company is a going concern or until the person in whose favour the charge is created intervenes;
- Preferential creditors take priority;
- Execution creditors may be able to seize assets before the bank has taken steps to protect its position;
- The most realisable assets have usually already been realised to stave off pressing creditors by the time the banker crystallises his charge;
- Certain "assets" may be subject to reservation of title and thus not be available to the debenture holder.

Registration of Charge:
under Section 95 Companies Act 1948 (Section 395 of the Companies Act 1985) all charges (with exceptions given below) created by a company are required to be registered with Registrar of Companies within 21 days of date of creation of charge.

(Exceptions are charges on stocks and shares, bills of exchange, life policies, produce).

Remedies of Debenture Holder:
On default any floating charge crystallises and:

- Bank can sue for repayment and enforce security by sale.
- Bank can appoint Receiver (as authorised under terms of usual bank debenture) or apply to court for one to be appointed. (Although not usual steps, bank could apply to court for foreclosure or present a winding up petition).

Appointment of Receiver:
Form of appointment drawn up by bank, executed on behalf of bank and handed to Receiver.

Appointment has to be registered with Registrar of Companies within 7 days. Powers of Receiver will be set out in bank's debenture.

Powers normally include power to carry on business of company, sell assets and virtually do anything incidental to achieving objective.

Receiver usually appointed as agent of company rather than bank to make company and not bank responsible for his acts and remuneration.

Application of proceeds of security:
Receiver has to pay regard to any rights of creditors or others with prior claims and also has a responsibility to unsecured creditors.

Statutory preferential creditors have to be paid before bank in respect of proceeds of assets which were subject to bank's floating charge.

Proceeds of any fixed charge security would go to bank (after satisfying any prior mortgages).

Floating Charge proceeds applied as follows:

(1) Costs of realisation of assets

(2) Costs and remuneration of receiver

(3) Amounts due to Preferential Creditors

(4) Bank's advance.

Receiver's Account:
Usually the receiver will require an account through which to collect proceeds of realisations and make necessary disbursements. Bank's form of mandate should be completed.

Sometimes receiver will need to borrow on the account — e.g. if trading, for wages and materials — and receiver would be personally liable for the debt, unless indemnified formally or otherwise by banker.

End of Receivership:
When receiver has realised all assets, paid off any prior mortgages and preferential claims, the amount he holds, less his own costs and remuneration, will be transferred to the company debt in reduction. Notice of the receiver ceasing to act will be given to the Registrar of Companies.

Question 40

A Limited company which banks with you has a substantial unsecured overdraft. Lately there have been excesses, and the company appears to be having some difficulty in operating within the limit. Upon enquiry you are told that these difficulties are due to labour trouble and are only of a temporary nature, but you feel

SECURITY FOR ADVANCES

that the time has come to secure the account. You are offered a debenture incorporating a floating charge over the company's assets and decide to accept it. (The company operates from rented premises and the plant and machinery, being of a specialised nature, will fetch little in a liquidation.)

What precautions are necessary in taking such security, and what dangers are there inherent in it?

[B]

Question 41

Wilkman Trading Company Ltd. have unsecured overdraft facilities at the West Bank Ltd. Limit £20,000. On January 3rd, their overdraft was £16,000 and on that date the bank agreed to grant a further advance by way of a Loan of £20,000 for a special purpose. A draft was issued by the bank for that amount and debited to a separate Loan Account in the Company's name. The Company gave the bank a specific charge by way of legal mortgage on its factory to secure the Loan only; and also gave a floating charge on all the other property of the Company to secure the bank, on the usual continuing security basis, in respect of the existing overdraft and any overdraft that might be permitted. The securities were taken on January 3rd, and between that date and August 3rd, £12,000 was paid into the current account and £15,000 out. The Loan remained unchanged. On August 3rd, the Company went into liquidation.

Discuss the bank's position in detail.

[B]

Question 42

Longs Concrete Products Ltd. entered into a contract with Bourne Corporation to supply a quantity of concrete blocks and obtained finance for the project from the Cornhill Bank Ltd. upon a separate loan account.

The managing director now tells you that the company cannot, by reason of its security when the loan was being negotiated, but, as repayment from the proceeds of the contract seemed assured, the bank did not insist upon taking any formal charge. It did, however, obtain and lodge with the Corporation an authority signed by the company, expressed to be irrevocable without the consent of the bank, instructing the Corporation to remit all monies due under the contract to Cornhill Bank Ltd., whose receipt would be a good discharge. The Corporation acknowledged these instructions and undertook to comply. Deliveries have been taking place under the contract for the past six weeks but no payments have yet been made by the Corporation.

The managing director now tells you that the company cannot, by reason of its liabilities, continue in business and that an early meeting is to be called to pass a resolution for voluntary winding up. He has every hope that all creditors will be paid in full within the next twelve months.

How is the bank affected?

[B]

Question 43

Arrow Valves Ltd., who have not previously needed to borrow from the bank, have approached you this week to discuss the possibility that with customers taking longer to settle their accounts, the company may during the coming months find itself with a liquidity problem of a temporary nature unless its suppliers can in turn be persuaded to extend longer credit. You are willing to help the company subject to provision of security and are asked to accept a floating charge over the assets of the company. This is to be held undated, and only dated and registered should it prove necessary to take bank borrowing: the directors feel that registration at this stage may affect their ability to negotiate extended terms with their suppliers. Explain how you would reply, giving your reasons.

[B]

Section 7
Security for Advances

TYPES OF SECURITY

TITLE DEEDS AND LAND CERTIFICATES

Unregistered land: title evidenced by documents known as title deeds.

Registered land: registered at Land Registry under Land Registration Act 1925; evidenced by a Land Certificate.

Two legal estates in land:

Freehold (or estate in fee simple)

Leasehold (or term of years absolute)

Leasehold Property as security:
Value depends upon:

    Length of lease
    Terms of lease
    Nature, condition and situation of property.

Generally, short term leases not good banking security; at end of period property reverts to lessor and may be claims for dilapidation arise. There could however be valuable options to renew.

Any leases have disadvantages:

- Property decreases in value as each year lessens length of lease.
- Ground Rent payable.
- Lease may contain onerous and restrictive covenants and breach of these may entail forfeiture.
- Underleasing may be prohibited.

Despite these factors, value of property and thus bank's security will depend very substantially on nature, condition and site.

Legal Mortgage:
is transfer by mortgagor of a legal estate in the land to mortgagee as security.

Equitable Mortgage:
is an agreement to execute a legal mortgage if and when called for. Can be created by mere deposit of title deeds, in case of both freehold and leasehold land. (Bankers nevertheless would normally effect by Memorandum of Deposit.)

Priorities of Mortgages:
Depends upon

- Holding deeds or land certificate.
- Notice of prior rights.
- Registration of charge where necessary.

UNREGISTERED LAND:

Registers are:
Land Charges Dept.
Local Land Charges Registers
(Registrar of Companies if appropriate)

Mortgagee who holds deeds does not need to register charge (unless given by company). Therefore, non-production of deeds could be danger sign as it would be constructive notice that property charged elsewhere.

Possession of title deeds thus very important for priority of all mortgages of unregistered land depends upon date of registration except where mortgage protected by deposit of deeds.

Searches:
Searches must be made:

Of Land Charges Registry at Land Registry.
At Local Authority for Local Land Charges.
(At Registrar of Companies if appropriate)

Registrations:
Registration should be effected as follows to ensure priority for bank's charge:

Legal or Equitable Mortgage where deeds held — only registration is at Registrar of Companies if by a company.

Legal Mortgage without deeds — In Land Charges Register as a land charge Class C (i) (Puisne mortgage)

Also if by company, register with Registrar of Companies.

Equitable Mortgage without deeds — In Land Charges Register as a land charge Class C (iii) (General Equitable Charge)

Also, if by company, register with Registrar of Companies.

Second Mortgages:
may be legal or equitable. Second mortgagee will not (usually) have the deeds; must therefore register charge as puisne mortgage.

Must also search to ensure no other mortgages outstanding.

Notice of Second Charge:
When bank receives notice of a subsequent charge, and if lending on current account,

the account should be broken to prevent operation of rule in Clayton's Case — *Deeley v. Lloyds Bank Ltd.* (1912).

REGISTERED LAND:

When land is registered, owner is entered on register and is issued with a land certificate in place of title deeds. This is evidence of title and transfer of title is effected by registration of new owner's name.

Land Register:

Comprises 3 parts

- Property Register
- Proprietorship Register
- Charges Register.

Legal Mortgage effected by bank's form of charge being sent to Registrar who in turn issues a Certificate of Charge on which will be details of prior charges and in which is bound the bank's charge. Registrar retains land certificate together with a copy of bank's charge.

Second Mortgage effected similarly with Certificate of Second Charge being issued.

Equitable Mortgage may be created by deposit of land certificate with or without memorandum of deposit. Notice of Deposit is sent to Registrar on special form and this acts as caution as Registrar has to give mortgagee notice of any proposed dealing with the property, enabling equitable mortgagee to take steps to protect his interests.

Searches and Registrations:
- Land Registry — registration made on production of land certificate but certain restrictions can be recorded e.g. creditor's notice following bankruptcy petition. (Notice of Deposit therefore needs to be given at time of search.) Official Search certificate can be obtained and, if clean, application for registration of charge within 15 days will get priority.
- Local Land Charges — as with unregistered land.
- Companies' Register — if appropriate.

Rights of Mortgagees:
Legal Mortgage

- Sue on personal covenant to repay
- Sell property
- Appoint Receiver of property
- Foreclosure
- Enter into possession

Equitable Mortgage
- Sue for payment
- Bring action to force mortgagor to execute legal mortgage
- Bring action for foreclosure
- Bring action for sale
- Apply to court for appointment of receiver.

Residential Properties as Security:
Following the "Boland" case (*Williams & Glyn's Bank Ltd. v. Boland* (1979)) banks and other lenders have had to consider whether any "Boland-type" equitable

interests in the property exist, and if so, the party(ies) concerned should either join in the charge (charging whatever interest they may have) or sign a disclaimer saying they have no interest. With residential property, particularly matrimonial homes, the question is of paramount importance.

Question 44

Your customer, Gerald Holmes, intends to buy a shop in a nearby village; he has just retired from his company and received a £12,000 gratuity which he will use towards the cost of buying the business. The household premises and goodwill are valued at £15,000 and the stock £4,200. He asks you for a loan of £8,000 against a charge over the leasehold deeds. The lease is for 21 years, of which eight have gone by. Required:

(i) Discuss the acceptability of the lease as security and;

(ii) Set out the procedure for completing the bank's charge by way of legal mortgage over the security.

[A]

Question 45

You are the securities officer at the No. 3 Grand Street branch of your bank and your manager has just passed you a copy note of a recent interview he has had. This reads:

Philip Morgan. — I have agreed in principle to a loan of £8000 repayable by monthly instalments over 4 years to assist with the purchase of a motorised caravan. Interest to be debited to current account. He has agreed to provide security but has few free assets. However five years ago he lent his company, Morgan Confectioners Ltd. (who bank with our City Branch) £20,000 to enable it to acquire its third retail shop, next door to us here at No. 5 Grand Street. He holds a charge certificate and he will do all that is necessary so that this security covers us.

Action: Securities Officer — please discuss security with me and let me know what steps are necessary to protect the bank. Are there any special points we should check before this lending is set up?

Required: Notes on the action you would take, giving your reasons.

[A]

Question 46

You have agreed to lend your customer, Owen Mosley £15,000 on a fluctuating basis to provide working capital for his tailoring business. As security you have asked Mr Mosley for a legal mortgage over his domestic property, which is now valued at £45,000. However, when the property was acquired by Mr. Mosley, he was assisted to the extent of £15,000 by a friend, with whom he lodged the Land Certificate as security. The friend, Mr. Donald Dodds acting on his solicitor's advice, lodged a notice of deposit at the Land Registry to protect his position.

Are there likely to be any special problems with the security offered and, if so, what can be done to overcome them? Give reasons for your answer.

[B]

SECURITY FOR ADVANCES

Question 47

Mr. Henshall, a wealthy customer, is borrowing £8,000 on a loan account which you agreed to enable him to add an extension to his home. The loan is being reduced at £250 per month and when it was granted in 1978 you were given a first legal mortgage by Mr. Henshall over the deeds of his house which you now value at £95,000. Mr. Henshall is a director of Steppingley Ltd., which also banks with you, and which from time to time borrows against Mr. Henshall's unlimited guarantee. Recent audited accounts for the company show that in the last twelve months it has traded at a loss, although its capital and reserves are still considered by you to be adequate for the lending of up to £60,000 on an occasional basis which you have permitted in the past.

Today, you have received a letter from Mr. Henshall saying that he wishes to transfer the deeds of the house into his wife's name, and he asks you to forward these to his solicitors, Hicks and Co., so that this can be arranged. You are prepared to agree, but wish the bank to continue to remain secured by the guarantee and the deeds.

Required: Notes on the considerations you would have in mind regarding your security. What would be the likely sequence of events, and how would you ensure that the bank was fully protected at all times?

[A]

Question 48

A. Bell has mortgaged the deeds of his house, worth £39,500, to the bank who have agreed to an overdraft limit of £16,000. When the account is £13,600 overdrawn at a later date, the bank receives notice that Bell has executed a second charge over the same property for £5,000 in favour of B. Young.

Outline the action, if any, the bank needs to take, giving reasons for your answer.

While the account is still £13,600 overdrawn Bell writes to the bank saying that as the form of charge he executed in favour of the bank was to secure "All monies due or to become due", and that as the arrangement agreed was for him to borrow up to £16,000 from the bank, he proposes to issue cheques for a further £2,400.

What should be the bank's reply?

[B]

Section 8
Security for Advances

TYPES OF SECURITY
GUARANTEES

Guarantee is an engagement to be collaterally answerable for debt, default or miscarriage of another person. Must be distinguished from an Indemnity which is a promise to be primarily liable.

Guarantee must be evidenced in writing — Section 4 Statute of Frauds 1677 — indemnity need not be.

Guarantee must be supported by consideration unless under seal — in bank guarantees consideration is usually "affording banking accommodation" or "continuing the account."

Guarantee not contract *Uberrimae Fidei* but banker must be careful not to run risk of charge of misrepresentation which could render contract voidable.

- *Disclosure to Prospective Guarantor*:
  Banker entitled to assume that guarantor has familiarised himself with the customer's financial position. Banker thus not bound to make any disclosure regarding customer's liabilities to bank.

  Relevant case law — *Hamilton v. Watson* (1845) and *Cooper v. National Provincial Bank Ltd.* (1945).

  If banker asked any questions any replies must be straightforward and if guarantor clearly under a misapprehension regarding debtor banker has duty to correct this — *Royal Bank of Scotland v. Greenshields* (1914). With regard to banker's duty of secrecy, bank should arrange for meeting of all parties, or obtain customer's written authority to disclose — *Westminster Bank Ltd. v. Cond* (1940).

  Customer should not be allowed to take guarantee form away for signature — risk of plea of *non est factum* — *Carlisle and Cumberland Banking Co. v. Bragg* (1911), although such plea now narrowed down considerably since *Saunders v. Anglia Building Society* (1970).

SECURITY FOR ADVANCES

- *Disclosure after guarantee signed*:
  Guarantor entitled to have details of his liability at any time — therefore if balance less than amount of guarantee he will be told that figure; if balance in excess of amount of guarantee, he will merely be told that guarantee fully relied upon.

  Banker need not advise guarantor of any change in debtor's position — *National Provincial Bank Ltd. v. Glanusk* (1913) — but if appropriate could threaten to call advance in unless guarantor put in picture.

Question 49

The East Bank Limited is pressing a customer to repay an overdraft of £3000 which is unsecured. The customer's father called at the bank and asked the manager, in the presence of the chief clerk, to delay proceeding for a few months during which time he would lodge the deeds of his house with the bank as security for his son's debt. This was agreed to and the deeds were duly deposited. No form of charge was taken, the manager relying on the supporting knowledge of the chief clerk of the oral arrangment. Six months later, no reduction having been made in the debt, the bank received a letter from the father's solicitors contending that "in the absence of consideration" their client was under no liability to the bank and they therefore requested the immediate return of the deeds. Give your opinion on this contention and discuss the bank's position with regard to the security.

[B]

Question 50

(a) A guarantor calls at the bank and asks to see a copy of the account which he guarantees. What should be your reply and why?

(b) A.B. agrees to guarantee the account of C.D. to the extent of £3000 to enable C.D. to buy additional stock for his retail toy shop for the forthcoming Christmas season. The guarantee is duly signed but a month later the banker realises that instead of buying stock, as was understood by the guarantor to be the purpose for which the guarantee was given, C.D. is using the accommodation for gambling. Should the banker advise the guarantor of this or take any action at all?

[B]

- *The Guarantor*:
  Any person with contractual power can normally give a guarantee.

- *Guarantee by Partnership*:
  Partner has no implied power to bind other partners — guarantee by one partner would bind other partners if clearly given in connection with firm's ordinary course of business.

  In practice, *all* partners should sign guarantee given by a firm.

- *Guarantee by company*:
  Company has no power to give guarantee unless such power expressly given in objects clause of its Memorandum of Association.

  Any power to give guarantees should be unambiguous.

  Articles of Association will set out extent to which such powers have been delegated to directors and will stipulate any special provisions as to manner in which guarantee is to be executed e.g. under seal or under hand.

Care needed to ensure that contract is between *company* and bank, and not directors and bank; this usually achieved by having covering board resolution endorsed on guarantee form itself.

- *Interested Directors*:
Resolution to give guarantee should be passed by independent quorum of directors, if any directors are personally interested in giving of the guarantee — *Victors v. Lingard* (1927).

If independent quorum not possible then company in general meeting should pass resolution.

- *Inter-company guarantees*:
It is quite common for parent companies to guarantee subsidiaries and vice versa, or for associated companies, to give guarantees for each other's liabilities.

In such cases (perhaps particularly when subsidiary guaranteeing parent) banker should invite directors to examine whether they consider it in interests of and of benefit to the "guarantor" company to enter into the guarantee. If they are of that opinion, then it should be reflected in the wording of the resolution. — *Charterbridge Corporation Ltd. v. Lloyds Bank Ltd.* (1969).

- *Guarantees by joint parties*:
If two or more persons are to give a joint guarantee, advance should not be made on strength of guarantee until all have signed — *National Provincial Bank Ltd. v. Brackenbury* (1906).

- *Independent Legal Advice*:
It is vital that a person is a free agent when entering into guarantee.

Lloyds Bank Ltd. v. Bundy (1974) threw a different slant on position, but nowadays banks increasingly are moving towards insisting on *all* guarantors (or indeed, all givers of third party security) having the benefit of independent legal advice.

Former practice was to take a "free will" clause where there could be "undue influence", but now tendency is to have all guarantors independently advised; the advising solicitor certifying to that effect on the guarantee form itself.

- *Bank Form of Guarantee*:
Drawn up to allow for a very wide range of what otherwise could be problems and is based on many years experiences.

Question 51

A prospective guarantor, having read the bank's form of guarantee, complains that it is too complicated for him to understand. He says however, that he is quite prepared to keep his promise to the principal debtor and is willing to act as surety for £1,000. He suggests that instead of signing the bank's form he should write a letter to the bank, undertaking to be fully responsible for any sums due to the bank from the principal debtor at any time up to a total of £1,000 if the debtor should fail to repay the bank, if required, on demand.

How would you regard this request if you were asked to make the decision?

SECURITY FOR ADVANCES

If you decided not to accede to the request, on what grounds would your refusal be based?

[B]

Question 52

Your customer, Alan Pearson, is overdrawn £4,000 and you have called on him to provide security. He telephoned last week to say that the only security available was a guarantee from his friend and business associate Tom Ryder, and that Mr. Ryder will call to see you shortly. In fact, Tom Ryder is already known to you, having been a customer himself for five years. He is a director of Ryder Construction Ltd. which banks at another of your branches. You consider him good for the liability.

In due course when Tom Ryder calls, he mentions that when he was first approached by Alan Pearson he had some reservations about signing a guarantee, but he now realises it is only a formality and he is therefore happy to sign. He mentions that he owes Alan Pearson £5,000 in respect of some sub-contracted work he has recently completed.

How would you react to this situation, and what action would you take? Give reasons for your answer.

[A]

- *Determination of Guarantee*:
  Guarantee determined by:

  - Guarantor giving prescribed notice and substantiating his liability.
  - Bank making formal demand.
  - Change of parties.
  - Death, mental disorder or bankruptcy of parties.

  Guarantee document will set out terms on which guarantor can determine. Period of notice stipulated; difficult position for banker once notice given as to whether he should permit borrowing to increase. Equitable solution is to consult both parties and come to an arrangement. On determination of guarantee, account should be broken to prevent Clayton's Case but some bank forms have a clause protecting bank if it fails to do this — such a clause was effective in *Westminster Bank Ltd. v. Cond* (1940).

- *Payments by Guarantor*:
  Any monies received from guarantor will be placed to a Suspense-type account, thus leaving banker free in subsequent event of customer's failure to prove for the full amount.

  Eventually, necessary amount to repay shortfall on debtor's account (or full balance of suspense account if needed) would be transferred to customer's account.

  Any surplus would be released to guarantor.

  Problem in practice can arise, where several separate guarantees have been substantiated and less than the total sum of these is needed. In such a situation, all banker can do is sit tight, but offer to transfer all the suspense balances into a separate account; from this account repay the principal debt and then release the surplus as instructed by all the guarantors jointly. On no account should banker be drawn into matter of how the individual guarantors sort out their positions at this stage.

- *Surrender of Guarantee Form:*
  Most bank guarantees stipulate that the guarantee remains property of bank, even when guarantor has discharged his liability. This can be important for first 6 months in case bank needs to have its rights under guarantee reinstated should fraudulent preference be held.

- *Determination by bank:*
  Limitation Act does not start to run against in guarantor's favour until demand made — *Bradford Old Bank v. Sutcliffe* (1918). Period is six years if under hand, twelve years if under seal.

- *Change of Parties:*
  Most bank guarantees provide that guarantee not affected by change in constitution of bank (e.g. by merger, take-over etc.).

  Additionally, guarantee should provide that it will be unaffected by change in constitution of firm, when guarantee given for partnership's liabilities.

- *Death of Guarantor:*
  Usual bank guarantee binds personal representatives; account need not therefore be broken but personal representatives of guarantor should be advised of the existence of the liability and terms under which they can give notice to determine.

- *Bankruptcy of Guarantor:*
  Account should be stopped and demand for repayment made; banker will prove against guarantor's estate in bankruptcy in respect of the contingent liability.

- *Bankruptcy of Debtor:*
  Stop account and make formal demand on guarantor; any moneys received from guarantor to be credited to Suspense-type account pending final outcome of principal debtor's bankruptcy.

- *Mental Disorder of Guarantor:*
  Account should be stopped as mentally disordered person's estate liable only for balance then due. Doubtful if a clause in guarantee purporting to make it effective as continuing security pending notice from Receiver would hold good.

Question 53

You have granted an overdraft to Mr. George Raymond against a guarantee covering all sums due to the bank from time to time, with a maximum amount of £2,000. The guarantee also contains a clause requiring three months' notice of determination. Today with the balance of Mr. Raymond's account £400 in credit, the guarantor advises you that he wishes his liability under the guarantee to cease as from next month.

What would be your reply?

[B]

Question 54

Your customer, Mr. Tom Reynolds owes the bank £1,100, which is only partly secured by a personal guarantee for £800 by Mr. Brian Eaves. The guarantee is on the bank's usual form.

You recently decided to make formal demand for repayment, and after receiving no satisfactory reply from Mr. Reynolds you made a demand on the guarantor Mr.

SECURITY FOR ADVANCES

Eaves does not wish to incur interest charges and sends you £800 in payment of his liability under the guarantee.

State what actions you would take and give your reasons.

[B]

Question 55

AB's account is secured by a guarantee for £1,000 given by CD, supported by a life policy for £2,000 on the life of CD and assigned by him to the bank. When AB's account is £750 overdrawn, CD dies. What action should the bank take

(a) With regard to AB's account;
(b) With regard to the guarantee; and
(c) With regard to the life policy?

[A]

Question 56

For several years Boden Company Ltd., has had an unsecured overdraft at your branch. Two years poor results have meant that when an application for renewal of the £75,000 overdraft facility was made 2 months ago you were requested by your head office to obtain some security. Company assets are not really satisfactory for the purpose but another company which banks with you, and has close trading links with Boden Company Ltd., has agreed to give a guarantee if you will continue the overdraft limit of Boden.

The proposed guarantor company, Aston Products Ltd., are Boden's main supplier; they are a first class company with a very sound account. The two companies have no directors in common, nor are there any inter-company shareholdings. Your head office accepts this offer.

What are the points that have to be examined, and what is the procedure for perfecting this security? Give reasons for your answers.

[B]

Section 9
Security for Advances

TYPES OF SECURITY

LIFE POLICIES:

If policy issued by first class British company and bank's security was properly taken, then no worry over payment if need arises to realise.

Insurance policy is contract uberrimae fidei which means insurance company could refuse to pay out if non-disclosure or misrepresentation occurred when proposal made.

Banker cannot do much to protect himself except check for any obvious discrepancy — admission of age important and if age not admitted, birth certificate should be sent to company for admission of age.

Bank should check for any restrictions and consider customer's lifestyle and activities in relation to these.

Essential to ensure that policy still in force; premium receipts should be obtained whilst policy held as security.

All beneficiaries of policy must join in charge; if any of beneficiaries are minors no charge will be effective.

Where beneficiaries are other than the assured, they should all be named with reasonable certainty to avoid possible problems — *Cousins v. Sun Life Assurance* (1932) and *Re Browne's Policy* (1903).

- *Industrial Policies*:
  are small policies where premiums often payable weekly and collected by agent. Have disadvantages as security as follows:
  - often assignable only under certain restrictions
  - carry relatively small surrender value
  - require frequent payment of premiums; possibly difficult to obtain satisfactory proof of payment.

SECURITY FOR ADVANCES

- *Surrender Value*:
  is what usually concerns lending banker primarily; this is amount the insurance company would pay out if policy surrendered.

  Capital value can be significant when banker lending essentially unsecured but where continued existence of customer is crucial to banker's source of repayment — e.g. when lending to professional partnership and firm's ability to repay rests on continued existence of partners.

- *Charges over Life Policies*:
  Can be legal or equitable mortgage (known as "assignment" with policies).

  Legal charge will allow for redemption and contain power for banker to surrender policy for cash or for fully paid policy or to sell the policy. Customer usually undertakes not to do anything to invalidate policy and bank's form will contain all usual banking clauses such as continuing security etc.

  Under Policies of Assurance Act 1867, insurance companies must accept written notice of assignment. Non-production of policy has been held to constitute notice of a prior charge — *Spencer v. Clarke* (1878).

  Bank therefore first obtains policy and ascertains from company whether any prior charges. Equitable charge can be taken by deposit of policy with or without a memorandum of deposit. Notice given to company who need not acknowledge equitable interests but usually do.

  Legal mortgagee can sell or surrender policy without reference to depositor or court; equitable mortgagee would have to go to court to realise security if chargor will not cooperate. If policy becomes claim, equitable mortgagee will require the personal representatives to join in discharge.

- *Loans on Policies by Insurance Company*:
  Most insurance companies will make loans within the surrender value of the policy and this can be a good way of banker obtaining repayment whilst at same time allowing customer to retain the cover.

PRODUCE AND MERCHANDISE ADVANCES

Drawbacks of produce and merchandise as security:

- liable to depreciation, special problems if perishable
- subject to varying market prices
- can only be realised by sale, often forced sale
- may be subject to charges for freight and storage
- property to goods will not pass unless documents of title delivered or goods warehoused in bank's name
- there is scope for fraud and security is never perfect.

Question 57

Your customers Trevor Potter and Arthur Askew traded as Continental Fruits and were importers of tinned fruit until they went into bankruptcy recently. Two years ago, when they had the opportunity of supplying a large foodstore chain on a regular basis, you advanced moneys to them as the foodstore chain insisted on taking six weeks credit between delivery of supplies and payment. The tinned fruit was to be imported from several European countries and you were told that the overseas exporters required early payment.

Because of the amounts involved, you asked for security but the only security the partners could give was a charge over the stocks of goods themselves held from time to time in warehouses to the order of the partnership. You accepted this position and took the usual steps to perfect your security.

Now, however, following the failure of the firm, you have heard from another bank, Atlas Financing Ltd., to the effect that Continental Fruits had an account with that bank and they claim to have a charge over a consignment of tinned fruit which you believed formed part of your security. These goods have been inadvertently released from the warehouse and pledged to Atlas Financing Ltd.

A German supplier has also written claiming that two of his consignments to Continental Fruits had not been paid for, and that he is therefore entitled to either the tinned fruit or the sale proceeds.

Required:

(a) a statement in note form, of the steps originally taken by the bank to perfect its security.

(b) Comments on the bank's position in respect of the claims which have now arisen.

[A]

AGRICULTURAL CHARGES

Form of security available only to banks — under Agricultural Credits Act 1928.

Is a charge on farming stocks and assets; charge can be fixed or floating or combination of both. Fixed charge covers that stock and assets belonging to farmer at date of charge and as specified in charge; floating charge covers stock and other assets from time to time belonging to farmer.

In event of default, fixed charge gives bank right to take possession of property; similarly bank can take this step on death or bankruptcy of farmer; if above events occur a floating charge would become fixed.

- *Bank Form of Charge*:
  The usual bank form of Agricultural Charge incorporates both a fixed and floating charge.

  Charge must be registered within seven days with Agricultural Charges Superintendent at Land Registry.

  Registration of charges are not published; therefore prior to taking charge bank will search to ensure there is no prior charge.

Question 58

John Mosley farms 900 acres of land which he rents at £17000 per annum from Lord Fenton. His account has been regularly overdrawn over the last five years, with the figures increasing in the last twelve months.

You have asked Mr. Mosley to come in to your branch to see you and to bring his own up to date figures for the farm business. He explains his problems to you and you are sufficiently satisfied with the explanation to continue assisting him, provided he can provide security.

SECURITY FOR ADVANCES

Mr. Mosley is willing to give you an agriculture charge (a floating charge) and an assignment over a life policy, shown in his own draft figures which he has brought with him and which are given below. You notice that the policy is drawn up under the provision of the Married Womens Property Act 1882.

Required: Tabulate all the steps necessary to take the securities, so as to protect the bank fully at all times. You should indicate the value of each item of security, as you would enter it in your records, giving reasons for your answer, and add any further comments which you feel may be pertinent.

JOHN MOSLEY — FARMER

Liabilities	£	Assets	£
Loans	10,000	Livestock	3,000
Rent due	4,250	Harvested Crops	78,000
Merchants, seedsmen	29,250	Growing Crops	18,600
Tax	7,000	Stores, foodstuffs, fertilizers	9,000
Life Policy Premium Arrears	400	Machinery/Tractors	10,500
Other creditors	12,100	Car	3,000
Bank overdraft	50,000	Debtors	29,400
	113,000	Life Policy £25000 surrender value	1,500
Capital	40,000		
	£153,000		£153,000

[A]

Section 10
Further Examination Questions

Question 59

You are the manager of a suburban branch of XYZ Bank PLC, a member of the London Bankers' Clearing House. The account of Mr. Bullen, one of your customers, regularly comes up on your morning computer refer list showing irregular accounts. Mr. Bullen has borrowing limits of £3000 on his current account and £8000 on his loan account and you have made it clear to him that these limits will be strictly enforced and that cheques will be returned if necessary to achieve this.

On this morning's refer list, the balances as at the close of business last night are shown as Current Account Dr £3,502 and the loan account Dr £8000. You ask to see the relative vouchers for yesterday to ascertain what entries have caused this position. Shortly after the bank has opened for business, your clerk tells you of the items debited in yesterday's general clearing:

(i) a crossed cheque in favour of A. Collins for £179 dated seven days ago;

(ii) a crossed cheque in favour of L. Brown for £41 dated two days ago, with Mr. Bullen's cheque card number 1320467 on the reverse;

(iii) a crossed cheque in favour of V. Johnston for £68 dated one month hence;

(iv) a direct debit for £39 in favour of Armstrong Assurance Company;

(v) an open cheque in favour of D. Barnes for £69 dated almost twelve months ago.

Your clerk also informs you that, at the counter today, a Mr. Moore has just tendered a bank giro credit for his account at your Town Branch for £200. This credit consists of cash together with a crossed cheque for £100 drawn by your customer, Mr. Bullen, and dated yesterday. Mr. Moore has asked if the cheque is paid.

Your clerk suggests that you dishonour all items. Bearing in mind that you do not wish to increase the bank's exposure, how would you reply to him and what instructions would you give? Give reasons for your answer.

[A]

FURTHER EXAMINATION QUESTIONS 63

Question 60

Plan Stars Ltd. is borrowing £100,000 from you against the security of a debenture given three years ago, which incorporates a fixed charge over its land and buildings and a floating charge over all other assets. At an interview with the directors, they tell you that the company is proposing to enter into a factoring agreement with Topline Funding Ltd. in order to assist its cash flow. The directors say that part of the arrangement will be that Plan Stars Ltd. will assign its existing and future book debts to the factoring company who will in future carry out all the company's bookkeeping and the collection of monies due to it.

How would the bank's position be affected and what arrangements would you make? Set out your points in the form of a tabulated answer.

[A]

Question 61

Hallows Ltd. has maintained a satisfactory account with you for 20 years. It has an overdraft limit of £100,000 secured by an unlimited debenture giving the bank a fixed charge over freehold premises (£75,000) and plant and machinery (£40,000), and a floating charge over the current assets — debtors (£150,000) and stock and work in progress (£50,000). The managing director tells you that, on the advice of accountants, Hallows Ltd. will become a holding company at the beginning of next month, and a new wholly-owned subsidiary company, (Hallows (Mark II) Ltd., has been incorporated to take over the trading. He asks you to open an account for Hallows (Mark II) Ltd. and grant the overdraft facility of £100,000 on this account with effect from the first of next month. No overdraft will be required for Hallows Ltd.. You agree to this request.

Set out the procedure you will follow in order to ensure that the bank retains the benefit of the existing security.

[A]

Question 62

Drax Micro Ltd. is a computer consultancy agency incorporated two years ago, which banks at your branch. The director and secretary are Mr. Rose and his wife respectively and the company trades from their home address, 41, High Street. The company has prospered but, because some customers are slow to pay, it requires occasional overdrafts of up to £20,000. Provided there is adequate security, the bank is prepared to help.

Unfortunately, 41, High Street is fully mortgaged and the company has no suitable assets of its own to charge. However, Mr. Rose has a good friend and neighbour who runs a market gardening business in the name of Valex Nurseries Ltd. which adjoins 41, High Street. Mr. Rose says that Valex Nurseries Ltd. is prepared to guarantee Drax Micro Ltd. and that the four acres of market-garden land can be mortgaged to the bank, but he is uncertain whether the land is in the name of Valex Nurseries Ltd. or Mr. Vernon (the owner and proprietor of the business) himself.

You are the securities officer at the branch, and your manager asks you to let him have your observations on the acceptability of the security offered, together with a note of any special aspects which need consideration. How would you respond?

[A]

Question 63

Greenfield Limited have banked with you for three years, and you know that the company has accounts with competitor banks.

At a recent interview you agreed to lend the company £30,000 repayable over five years, to assist with the building of an extension to their existing factory premises, provided adequate security was lodged.

The two directors accepted your need for security, but said that they were anxious to retain a degree of flexibility in case they should need to borrow from their other bankers in the future. Consequently, they would give you only either a first mortgage over the company's existing leasehold land and buildings, valued at £40,000 in the company's last balance sheet, or their joint and several guarantee for £30,000, supported by two second mortgages, equity £20,000 in each, over their matrimonial homes, title to which is in their sole name in each case. They say that they will in any event agree to postpone their loans of £10,000 each to the company in favour of the bank.

Required: Tabulate the attractions and disadvantages of each of the securities offered, and say what further information you might require, if any, to enable you to reach your decision.

[A]

Question 64

Birchgate Homes Ltd. ceased trading last year, but was not placed into liquidation as it had no assets apart from a plot of building land which was mortgaged to the bank. With the assistance of estate agents, the bank sold this land for £20,000 which left a residual borrowing of £5000. The bank then called upon the guarantor, Len Hunt, to meet his liability, and informed him that interest would accrue on his liability until repayment.

Today you have received a letter from him saying that he cannot understand how he has any liability to the bank. He says that if legal proceedings are taken he will dispute the claim on the grounds that he is no longer associated with the company as he resigned as a director six months ago, when the bank took it upon itself to sell the company's asset. In any event, he alleges, the bank has sold the land for too low a price, and if it had obtained £25000, the valuation in the company's balance sheet, the bank would have been fully repaid. He goes on to say that he never agreed to pay interest, and was not allowed to consult his solicitor when he executed the guarantee in 1974.

What is the bank's position, and how would you respond to Mr. Hunt's letter?

Give reasons for your answer.

[A]

Question 65

In 1977 Mr. Victor and Mr. Alliss formed a limited company, Victall Electronics Ltd., to develop and manufacture electronic instruments. Mr. Victor and Mr. Alliss became directors and each held 40% of the equity capital. The private and company accounts are all at your branch, and are overdrawn. As security for the company borrowing, you hold an unlimited joint and several guarantee given by Mr. Victor and Mr. Alliss in 1977. For Mr. Victor's own borrowing (granted in 1980) and liabilities generally you were given a share certificate over 17,500 shares in Victall Electronics Ltd. in Mr. Victor's name, lodged without any other documentation. Mr. Alliss secured his borrowing when you first granted an overdraft in 1976, by handing you a life policy for £25,000 payable at death.

Mr. Victor recently called to see you and said that the shares of Victall Electronics Ltd. were to be introduced onto the unlisted securities market, with a view to the further growth of the company. He expected the company's borrowing to be reduced over the next six months from a number of sources. However, he asked you to increase his own borrowing so that he could buy 10% of Mr. Alliss' shares. You agreed to his request and these shares would also be lodged with you as security.

Required:

(i) Tabulate notes on the nature, advantages and disadvantages of the various forms of security held by the bank prior to the recent interview with Mr. Victor.

(ii) Notes on any differences in the bank's security which would result from the development mentioned by Mr. Victor.

[B]

Question 66

Mr. John Beaumont is an antique dealer and has been known to his bank for three years. The account was satisfactorily conducted at first but the branch noticed that he started to draw against uncleared items, the total of which increased as time went on. The bank started to scrutinise all transactions on his account and found that some of the cheques he paid in were drawn on an account at another bank and that he signed alone on that account. Since he seemed to be using the clearing system to finance his business, the manager called him in to discuss the matter with him in order to ascertain whether the situation had arisen innocently or not.

Set out what you regard as the dangers of the practice referred to in the question and how these can best be dealt with?

[B]

Question 67

Camelot Gardens Limited is borrowing £8000 from you on a fluctuating overdraft and, as security, you hold an unlimited joint and several guarantee by Mr. Gray and his wife, supported by a legal charge from Mr. Gray over a life policy for £20,000 on his own life. The policy has a surrender value of £4,600. Mr. Gray is a director of the company, and Mrs. Gray is the secretary and a director.

You have just learnt that Mr. Gray has been killed in a road accident.

Required:

(i) Comments on the action you would take to protect the bank's position as regards its security, and other steps you would put in hand over the next few weeks.

(ii) A note of any differences in procedures which would now apply if the life policy had been taken out by the company on Mr. Gray's life.

[B]

Question 68

A manufacturing company banking with you currently has an overdraft facility of £100,000 secured by a first charge over the deeds of a small freehold property valued at £30,000, together with a floating charge. Over the last 18 months the company has suffered from the recession and, although in the past it traded profitably, it is now faced with very difficult trading conditions. The overdraft has been pressing against the limit for the past few months but the company has slimmed down its operation considerably so that the cost of the operation is now just about on a par with profitability arising from its sales. The bank feel that, given a fair wind, the company may survive but its financial position is precarious due to the significant losses it sustained and the effect these have had on the company's balance sheet. The bank is however willing to continue its support but wishes to protect itself as far as possible and, for that reason, intends to insist on the opening of a separate wages account to which is to be debited money advanced for the payment of wages and salaries.

How does the bank obtain an advantage by this action, and what are the general considerations surrounding the opening and operation of a wages account?

[B]

Section 1

Answers

Answer 1

A banker's duty of secrecy to his customer is a legal duty implied in the contractual relationship between banker and customer, and information may be divulged only in the four instances set out in *Tournier v. National Provincial & Union Bank* (1924) viz. (1) under compulsion of law; (2) under a public duty; (3) where the interests of the bank require disclosure; and (4) where made by the express or implied consent of the customer. In practice, these instances are very rare and in most cases a bank is not in a position to give details of a customer's account to a third party, and in neither (a) nor (b) should any disclosure have been made.

(a) Here the police officer ought to be told that the bank cannot supply him with the information he is seeking without the express permission of the customer, or unless so directed by a court order. Doubtless the bank would want to be as helpful as it could, and could therefore undertake to contact its customer and ask him to get in touch with the police.

In any event, the bank should have acted when the first cheque so signed was presented and returned, and ascertained from the customer how these cheques had come to be issued and presented. Presumably the cheques have been lost or stolen and thus the situation should be clarified immediately with Mr. Johnson. Certainly, the bank needs to exercise care, and if it becomes apparent that legal proceedings could arise, the customer's written authority must be taken to disclose any information that may be asked for by third parties. The question does not indicate whether or not the cheques purported to have been drawn under a cheque card, but if the traders concerned accepted cheques, presumably from people they did not know, without insisting upon the production of a cheque card, they do seem to have taken an unnecessary risk in this day and age and, if they end up losing money, the blame must fall substantially on their own doorsteps. The bank's records should be marked so that any further cheques presented for payment on the account are carefully examined and, if necessary, returned with a similar answer.

(b) Here again, unless the customer provides the bank with a written authority to send copy statements to the police, the bank cannot comply with the police officer's request. In the absence of such authority the police ought to arrange to subpoena the bank under the Bankers Books Evidence Act 1879, the Act allowing for copies of entries to be produced and not the actual ledgers or ledger sheets.

Answer 2

As in the preceding question, the issue again is whether or not the bank can disclose information to outside parties, and therefore the circumstances in each situation need considering in relation to the "Tournier" Case.

(a) The question here is whether the enquiry from the Inland Revenue falls within the exception of "compulsion of law" under the "Tournier" case. It should also be remembered that under Section 20 Taxes Management Act 1970 (as amended by the Finance Act 1976) the Inland Revenue has extensive powers to investigate. Consequently, if the letter received was a request under this Section, despite Mr. Wyatt's strict instructions which had bound the bank to a specific contract of secrecy rather than an implied one, nevertheless it would be incumbent upon the bank to answer. The customer should naturally be advised of this and the situation explained to him. If the letter did not fall within this section at the present stage, the bank should not reply without the customer's written authority which it should have sought.

(b) Despite the fact that the bank will obviously wish to be as helpful as it can to its important company customer and will also be attracted by the thought of opening a number of new accounts, it would not be right for the bank to comply with the request. Although the information asked for may seem innocuous and the danger of any backlash to the bank may seem remote, the position remains that the bank would be out of order in disclosing to the company the names of those employees who had accounts, without the authority of those employees. The practical solution would be for the company to circularise its staff and ask them if they already have bank accounts and, if so, where.

Answer 3

This question concerns the bank's right of set-off and this is an area which can cause problems for a banker when he has been relying on a credit balance as offsetting an overdrawn balance on another account and then finds himself faced with a cheque drawn on the credit account. Case law remains somewhat unclear on this topic but for set-off to occur at all, the debt must be (a) an ascertained sum, (b) due to and by the same parties and (c) in the same right.

In *Garnett v. McKewan* (1872) it was held that the right of set-off could be exercised without notice but some doubt was cast on this in *Greenhalgh v. Union Bank of Manchester* (1924) where there was an inference that the mere fact that separate accounts had been opened constituted an implied agreement to keep them separate. Such doubts were however laid to rest in *National Westminster Bank Ltd. v. Halesowen Presswork and Assemblies Ltd.* (1972).

In the situation outlined in the question, the bank clearly has no right of set-off over the partnership account which is not in the same name or same right as the debt. Furthermore, the beneficial interest in the account may well belong solely to the brother as stated.

As regards the credit balance on the No.2 account, the most likely view is that the bank is now precluded from exercising a right of set-off, on the grounds that it is now fixed with notice of a trust. The bank could "grasp the nettle" and set-off this credit balance but could in doing so expose itself to an action if it later has to return a cheque drawn on the No.2 account. Another problem is that if the bank asks Ball for proposals for repaying his No.1 account, this could clearly be construed as admission on the part of the bank that it has no right of set-off, and therefore the bank really has to decide which course it is to adopt and then stick to it.

There certainly must be no delay if the bank is to reject Ball's effort to fix the bank with notice of trust as regards the No.2 account balance; the bank, if it decides to go down this route, should immediately formally advise Ball that the balance on the No.2 account is not withdrawable as the bank has been relying on it as set-off for the overdrawn No.1 account and is now crystallising the right of set-off. On balance it is unlikely that the bank would be safe in attempting to set-off the No.2 account balance and therefore the most proper course for it to take would be to acknowledge the existence of the "trust."

Ideally, the bank should have written to Ball as soon as the No.1 account became overdrawn and told him that this had been permitted in reliance on the credit balance on the No.2 account and that the latter balance (or the appropriate portion of it) was therefore no longer withdrawable. The bank should have at that stage asked Ball to make a transfer or to come in to discuss the situation. Letters of set-off are often taken by banks but would not normally be taken in a case involving small balances such as in this question or in cases where accounts are merely designated "No.1 a/c" "No.2 a/c" etc.

Obviously, if the bank decides to accept that the No.2 account is unavailable to it, then the bank can only seek Ball's proposals for repaying and perhaps securing the £1300 overdraft. The bank would doubtless be very keen to be furnished with satisfactory evidence of the travel club and its entitlement to the balance, and to ensure that the £1600 was paid over to a travel agent.

Answer 4

As far as Mr. Cox is concerned, the bank has made a mistake and quite clearly has disobeyed his express instructions. He must therefore be refunded immediately with £1750 and initially the bank should debit this to a suspense account. The question does not indicate that any cheques drawn on Cox's account have been returned unpaid for lack of funds over the past few months, but if this had been the case, the position of the bank could be more serious since Cox's credit could have been damaged. However, the latter would doubtless have brought the error to light at an earlier stage. The fact that a statement was sent to Mr. Cox is unlikely to help the bank since it is generally still considered that a customer is not under a legal obligation to examine his statement.

Similarly the bank could be in a very weak position as far as Mr. Cox's wife is concerned unless the bank can prove that she was aware of the "stop" and took advantage of the bank's mistake. If she has acted honestly the bank, having misled her, would be estopped from denying that funds were received for her credit — *Lloyds Bank Ltd. v. Brooks* (1950) and *United Overseas Bank v. Jirwani* (1976).

Other relevant cases are *Skyring v. Greenwood and Cox* (1825) and *Holt v. Markham* (1923).

In the "*Jirwani*" case it was outlined that the following three conditions must be met before a customer could resist repayment: (a) that the bank had misrepresented the state of his account, (b) that he had been misled by the misrepresentation and (c) that as a result he had changed his position in a way which would make it inequitable to require him to repay the money.

It may be, of course, that the funds wrongly paid over are still in Mrs. Cox's account and that she will acknowledge the position and return the £1750.

Answer 5

LIEN is the right of one person to retain that which is in his possession belonging to another until a debt due from the latter is paid.

PARTICULAR LIEN is such a right to retain goods *in respect of which the debt was incurred*; e.g. a watchmaker has a lien on a watch left with him for repair in respect of the cost of the repairs effected.

GENERAL LIEN is the right to retain goods not only in connection with the particular debt incurred in relation to them but also for the general balance owing by their owners to the person exercising the lien; e.g. a stockbroker would have a general lien on securities which, having been purchased by him for a client, were still in his possession and the client owed for other purchases made.

BANKER'S LIEN is a special form of general lien for it includes a right of sale over negotiable securities after reasonable notice. It is the right of a banker to retain in his possession until a debt due to him from a customer has been paid, such securities belonging to that customer as come into the banker's hands *in the ordinary course of his business as a banker* unless there is an express or implied contract to the contrary; e.g. bills and documents left for collection are part of the banker's ordinary business and he would have a lien on a bill left for collection by a customer whose account was overdrawn. It should be noted that the general interpretation of a banker's right of sale is that it refers only to *negotiable* securities. Reasonable notice would need to be given to the customer.

A banker's lien has been defined as an "implied pledge" — *Brandao v. Barnett* (1846) in relation to negotiable securities.

(i) A banker would not have a lien over deeds left accidentally on the counter by a customer when paying in a credit as the deeds would not have come into the banker's possession *in the ordinary course of his business as a banker*.

(ii) If securities are left at the bank by a customer who stated that the bank should retain them as security for his overdraft, these oral instructions constitute an equitable mortgage by deposit and therefore the question of lien does not arise.

(iii) If securities are deposited for safe custody, in other words, if they come into the banker's hands in his capacity as *bailee* and not in the ordinary course of his business *as banker* this would be a contract inconsistent with lien. Lien would, therefore, not arise.

Answer 6

In the situation given in this question, the certificates should be given up to the nephew only on the express authorisation of Bennett for the bank's primary responsibility is to the person in whose name they are deposited. The fact that the share certificates are registered in the nephew's name does not entitle him to withdraw them in the absence of instructions from the depositor. Indeed it could well be that the certificates are in the uncle's possession (via the bank) for a specific purpose e.g. as "security" given by the nephew in respect of a loan made to him by his uncle and this demonstrates why serious problems could face the banker if he released goods to a party other than the depositor.

If in the situation given, there is nothing sinister behind the nephew's request then a suitable authority from his uncle should be readily forthcoming. If on the other hand, there is a dispute and the nephew claims that the certificates must not be given back to his uncle, then the bank's only safe course would be to refuse to release the certificates without directions from the court, in the absence of a discharge from both the uncle and nephew.

Answer 7

The bank is in a very weak position here since, although Rogers had authorised his secretary to deal with his safe custody box, this was only to have access in order to list the contents and the bank should have ensured that a bank officer remained with the secretary while she examined the items in the box. The question whether the bank is a paid or gratuitous bailee is not directly relevant here, and although Rogers can claim on his insurance company (providing of course he has appropriate cover) there would seem to be a real likelihood that the insurance company would be able to stand in Rogers' shoes and bring an action against the bank for breach of its duty of care. As regards the likely success or otherwise of the claim, the bank will have no real ground for defending an action, whereas if a bank officer had remained with Rogers' secretary there seems little doubt that the bank could have defended the action successfully. If Rogers is a good customer of high standing and of value to the bank, the bank should consider the possibility of trying to reach a friendly settlement particularly since this would benefit both parties by saving the legal costs of bringing and defending an action.

Answer 8

The bank would not be in order in accepting Barber's instructions for the disposal of the sealed envelope upon his death since all mandates would be cancelled by his death, including this authority. The title to the envelope would then pass to Barber's legal personal representative(s) whose discharge would be the only discharge acceptable to the bank, and even then only after the production of probate or letters of administration.

Barber seems to be trying to make a disposition of his property in the event of his death instead of leaving it to Jones in his will, but such an attempt to by-pass his personal representatives should not be countenanced by the bank. Alternatively the envelope could contain Barber's will but if this is the case then there should not need to be any secrecy on the part of Barber as to the contents of the envelope and if the envelope was deposited with the bank for safe keeping, perhaps marked "Will of _____ Barber", it would be opened upon the depositor's death in the presence of interested parties but would be released by the bank only to the executor(s) named in the will or to the solicitors acting for the executor(s).

The banker quite clearly therefore will need to go into this request from Barber more fully but must guard against accepting any arrangement which will be storing up problems for the bank in the future.

If a banker accepts items for safe custody, he is bound to deliver them to the person who entrusted them to him. If he delivers them to the wrong person he is liable for conversion. A person is guilty of conversion if, being in possession of goods, he deals with them in a manner that deprives the rightful owner of dominion over them (*Hiort v. Bott* (1874)).

Section 2

Answers

Answer 9

It is not uncommon for bankers when lending to limited companies to request that the directors show their faith in their own company by giving their personal guarantee for the company's account. The practice has much to commend it, but it should be remembered that by reason of their liability under the guarantee the directors are *personally* interested and there is consequently a possibility of the security being upset on a liquidation should *they have committed any voluntary act which would benefit them to the detriment of other creditors* of the company — in other words, if there should be fraudulent preference.

In the example given in the question, it is clear that at the 10th May, when A.B. commenced to reduce the bank overdraft and ceased paying trade accounts, he was aware that the Company was insolvent, having been so informed by the Company's accountants early in that month. No pressure had been exerted by the bank for repayment so that no question of duress could arise. It follows therefore that by repaying the bank so as to obtain the release of his guarantee he was fraudulently preferring the bank to the other creditors *in order to benefit himself* at their expense.

A somewhat similar position arose in the case *Re M. Kushler* (1943) where a director, being aware of his responsibility under a guarantee for his company so conducted the company's business that he realised enough to repay the Company's Account. On the subsequent liquidation of the company the Court upheld the liquidator's contention that the procedure was a fraudulent preference and the bank concerned had to refund certain of the payments in and, moreover, was not allowed credit for items paid out during the period starting when the preference of the bank had commenced.

The facts outlined in (ii) of the question (as do those in (iii)) strengthen the view that in the instance outlined A.B. deliberately intended that his guarantee liability should be hidden from the general creditors.

The Meeting of the Creditors should by statute have been advertised in the London Gazette and at least two local papers, and it is unlikely that the bank could have remained ignorant of the position longer than a few days, depending on the time the advertisement was made, even although no notice of the Creditors' Meeting was sent to the Bank. Apart from that, of course, the paying in of credits and the lack of withdrawals ought to have been a danger signal to the Bank and put them on enquiry.

It seems clear that the Liquidator can claim from the bank all the items paid in to the Company's account since 10th May as on that date, the Company being insolvent, the fraudulent preference commenced.

Section 321 of the Companies Act 1948, however, includes a clause designed to protect bankers in such cases. It provides that where, in a winding-up, there has been a fraudulent preference of a person interested in security charged to secure the Company's account, the person preferred shall be subject to the same rights as if he had been personally liable to the extent of his interest. It would appear, then, that A.B. could thus be joined with the bank in any proceedings brought by the liquidator, the bank's right against him as surety being thus fully reinstated.

Answer 10

The vital point here is that a Receiving Order has been made against Gray and notice of this has reached the bank. A Receiving Order commences from the first moment of the day on which it is made and has the effect of making the Official Receiver the receiver of the debtor's property and thus the only person who can deal with the debtor's assets. The bank gets no protection under Sections 45 and 46 of the Bankruptcy Act 1914 once a receiving order has been made and the customer's account must be stopped completely.

The bank therefore in the case in question cannot permit any transactions through Gray's account.

The following should apply:

(a) The cheque for £340 in the clearing should be returned unpaid with the answer "Refer to Drawer" or "Receiving Order made". The fact that the cheque is dated prior to the making of the receiving order is immaterial.

(b) The bank cannot cash the cheque for £150. The question of living expenses is one which Gray will have to resolve with the Official Receiver.

(c) The salary credit when received must be retained and held to the order of the Official Receiver.

(d) The standing order cannot be paid.

(e) The bank was not affected as regards permitting transactions on Gray's account merely by judgement being made against Gray. The bank had no notice of an act of bankruptcy and will therefore be protected for the payments referred to by Section 45 of the Bankruptcy Act 1914.

Most banks have some system whereby all branches receive copies of "Stubbs" gazette or its equivalent, which list details of judgements, receiving orders, mortgages registered etc. Obviously when a customer's name is revealed showing judgement against that customer the fact should be noted by the bank and the bank is suitably alerted. However, this itself would not constitute an act of bankruptcy and the bank was therefore safe in making the payments stated in the question.

On a practical note, Gray should contact the Official Receiver without delay in order to resolve the urgent problems now facing him and to have the whole situation clarified.

SECTION 2: ANSWERS

Answer 11

Notice to creditors of suspension of payment of debts is an act of bankruptcy and the notice need not be in writing. It is sufficient if the language used is such as to lead any reasonable person to suppose that the debtor intends to suspend payment. Thus Hall, by giving notice to one of his creditors as stated in the question, that he is about to suspend payment of his debts, commits an act of bankruptcy.

Until a banker receives notice of an act of bankruptcy he can safely make and receive payments on the debtor's account as long as a Receiving Order has not been made (Section 45 of the Bankruptcy Act 1914) and Hall's account therefore could be conducted in the normal way until 5th February.

Upon receipt of notice of an act of bankruptcy, however, the position changes and payments or delivery of property are protected only if made to the debtor himself or to a person claiming by assignment from him (Section 46). From 5th February, therefore, payment should have been made only to Hall against the existing balance. A cheque in this country is not deemed to be an assignment of funds in the hands of the drawer, consequently no cheques to third parties would be paid. (This latter point is arguable — *Re Dalton* (1962) somewhat skirts round the specific issue — but the safe course is to regard third party cheques as not gaining protection under Section 46.)

Credits, if any, should be credited to a Suspense Account for three months, under advice to the customer, in case they should later be claimed by the Trustee in Bankruptcy when he is appointed as his title to such items relates back to the first available act of bankruptcy committed within three months prior to the presentation of the Petition.

Securities held for safe custody or otherwise should not, after notice of the act of bankruptcy, be delivered to anyone but the debtor himself.

The position changed again on 23rd April when the Receiving Order was made. From this date the account should have been stopped as from that time (i.e. the date of the Receiving Order) the Official Receiver or the Trustee in Bankruptcy are the only persons who can give an effective discharge to the bank for any balance or securities held.

The Official Receiver (or Trustee) would be advised of the position of the account and would, as he is so entitled to do, request the bank to pay over the credit balance remaining on the account and to deliver any property or securities of the debtor's held by the bank.

Had the account of Hall been overdrawn, the banker would in no circumstances, after receipt of notice of the act of bankruptcy have paid any cheques, since any surplus security held at the time the act of bankruptcy was committed might have become the property of the Trustee by virtue of the doctrine of "relation back". (Had the account been unsecured, any additional debt created after notice of the act of bankruptcy would not rank for proof against the debtor's estate. Any credits paid in would have to go to a separate Suspense Account and could not be drawn against.)

Answer 12

There is no legal decision which has settled this particular issue and therefore it is necessary to relate the facts to the law generally. As far as the branch is concerned, it must have seemed to be a fair solution to the problem to debit the cheques to the customer's account since the bank had no alternative but to pay the cheques which were issued prior to the making of the receiving order and drawn under the protection of the cheque card. The problem is whether or not the bank can exercise its right of set off in respect of a debt primarily arising under a separate contractual obligation from that which exists between the bank and its customer. Under the normal banker/customer relationship any cheque drawn on the account and presented after the receiving order had been made, would rightly have been returned by the bank with the answer "Refer to Drawer" or "Receiving Order made . . .", if the cheques had not been drawn in conjunction with the cheque card. (This would be so irrespective of the dates on the cheques.) However, as they were drawn under the cheque card scheme, a further relationship, under which the bank guarantees payment of the cheques to retailers, arises. In respect of this liability, the bank will have an implied indemnity from its customer. The question therefore is whether the bank is entitled to set off the sum it has paid under its guarantee, because of this right of indemnity. At the time of the receiving order, the bank's liability under the cheque card guarantee was contingent and apart from the existence of the receiving order there would have been no liability since there were sufficient funds available to meet the debt.

Section 30 of the Bankruptcy Act 1914 provides that all debts and liabilities present, future, certain or contingent are provable in a bankruptcy. Section 31 provides that before any such debts may be "set off" there must have been mutual dealings. The term "mutual dealing" has been given a wide construction by the courts; for example, it has been held that where a debt was not ascertainable at the date of the receiving order that it is "quite sufficient if the account can be taken when the set off arises", provided there have been "mutual dealings" between the debtor and the person claiming the set off at the date of the receiving order (*Re Daintray* (1900)).

Therefore, it is reasonable to submit that the bank is justified in seeking to set off the sum of £500 against the credit balance on Mr. Manley's account.

Answer 13

(a) On receipt of notice that a Receiving Order has been made against the bank's customer, Meredith, the bank will, of course, stop his account completely. As this leaves a debit balance of £10,400 against security valued at £9,200 the bank must then decide what course of action it shall take as regards proof. There are four courses open to a secured creditor:

 (i) He can give up his security and prove for the whole debt. (This is very rarely adopted as it would obviously be foolish to give up security in exchange for a dividend).
 (ii) He can realise the security and prove for any remaining debt.
 (iii) He can estimate the value of the security and prove for any remaining debt after deducting the assessed value.
 (iv) He can rely on his security and waive his right to prove. (This would not be a usual course to adopt).

Thus, in practice the choice is between (ii) and (iii). Realisation is preferable, but if a sale cannot be effected by the time it becomes necessary to submit the bank's proof for dividend purposes, then valuation should be adopted, in which case the Trustee may wish to redeem the security at the estimated value, the bank having the option of accepting the money or of submitting an amended proof. So far as the life policy is concerned, realisation is easy and will bring in the estimated (i.e. surrender) value, and as there is not likely to be much difficulty over the value of

SECTION 2: ANSWERS

the house, it is probably immaterial whether course (ii) or (iii) is followed, the bank thus proving for the shortfall of £1200.

The Trustee may assist the bank by including any property at the bank's disposal in a sale he may have arranged for other property of the debtor as he will be anxious to get the best possible price and so benefit all the creditors.

(b) Here again, on receipt of notice of the Receiving Order the bank will stop the account. As far as Meredith's estate in bankruptcy is concerned, the bank debt of £10,400 is unsecured and thus the bank will advise the official receiver or Trustee of the debt including interest and charges up to the date of the Receiving Order.

The bank will, of course, submit whatever proof of debt forms the Trustee may call for. The bank should make formal demand on Jones to substantiate his guarantee liability to the full extent of £9000 and should draw Jones' attention to the fact that interest will under the terms of the guarantee (provided that the usual form of guarantee taken by banks is held) run against him until such time as he substantiates his liability. (Some bank guarantees state that interest commences to run against the guarantor from the date the guarantee is called in, others stipulate that interest will run against guarantor from date of default by principal debtor, irrespective of whether or not the bank makes demand on the guarantor at that stage.) Any moneys received from Jones, should be placed to the credit of a suspense account and interest would normally be credited to these funds at the same rate that the principal debtor's account is being charged interest; alternatively the interest on the amount provided by Jones could merely be regarded as cancelling out the corresponding debit interest on the principal debt. When Meredith's bankruptcy has been completed and a final dividend paid, the bank will transfer the £9000 (or such lesser appropriate sum if the dividend has reduced the principal debt below £9000) out of the suspense account in repayment. Any surplus would be returned to Jones.

Answer 14

Under the Deeds of Arrangement Act, 1914, a deed of arrangement is void unless registered with the registrar of bills of sale within seven clear days of its execution. It will also become void unless, before or within 21 days after it has been registered or within such extended time as the court may allow, it has received the assent of a majority in number and value of the creditors. The assent of the creditor must be first established by his executing the deed or by sending to the trustee his written consent attested by a witness. A creditor holding security upon the debtor's property can only be reckoned as a creditor for the balance after deducting the value of the security. Creditors for sums not exceeding £10 are reckoned in the majority in value but not in number. A deed of arrangement is only binding on those who assent to it, but a trustee may serve on any creditor who has not assented a written notice of the execution of the deed and, if he does not reply within a month, then the deed cannot be used as an act of bankruptcy and it becomes binding on the dissentient creditor. If bankruptcy intervenes the deed becomes void, and those creditors who assented can, if they wish, present their own petition in bankruptcy based upon the deed of arrangement.

The action to be taken is as follows:

(1) When the notice from the solicitors is received, as it relates specifically to the customer's account, no further payments must be permitted.

(2) The branch manager should satisfy himself that the deed has been duly registered.

(3) It should be ascertained that the necessary assents have been received and that the deed has not become void for any reason.

(4) The balance can be paid to the trustee, whose discharge will be good, provided that a receiving order has not been made and that the banker has not had notice of a bankruptcy petition.

Section 3

Answers

Answer 15

Care is needed here and the bank should explain tactfully to Mr. Robins that a cheque book cannot be issued until certain formalities have been attended to; which may involve either the taking and following-up of satisfactory references and/or making credit searches/status queries through one or more credit reference bureaux. (Some banks have dispensed with the need to take references as part of their standard procedures and instead settle for seeing reasonable evidence of identification and search for any "adverse" information at one of the several leading credit-reference bureaux.)

The £300 cash could be provisionally accepted and Mr. Robins should be asked if he knows anyone who is known to the bank, whom the bank could perhaps contact by telephone to expedite things for him. If not, then the bank's formal procedures will have to be followed and Mr. Robins must await the outcome. A great deal of tact will be needed to ensure no offence to Mr. Robins and to avoid setting off on the wrong foot with a potential customer who may well have approached the bank as a result of its advertising.

Although some banks have decided to dispense with references as a general rule, failure to take suitable references can have serious consequences, not only for a bank but for the general public and possibly other banks should a person obtain a cheque book and then immediately start to misuse it. Since Mr. Robins is offering cash at this stage there is initially no risk of conversion as there could well be if he was trying to open the account with a cheque. Failure to take references was held to constitute negligence in *Ladbroke v. Todd* (1914) so depriving the collecting banker of his statutory protection under S.4 of the Cheques Act 1957 (then S.82 of the Bills of Exchange Act 1882).

Answer 16

The first point to recognise here is that the bank would appear to have acted incorrectly when they transferred the balance of Rose Burton's account into her husband's name without proper authority. Mental incapacity is governed by the Mental Health Act 1959 and under this a person may be compulsorily admitted to a hospital or recognised nursing home on a certificate signed by two doctors, or an application similarly supported may be made to the local health authority asking for a guardian to be appointed. In the event of either of these circumstances, the customer can be regarded by the banker as mentally incapable and the Act provides for the Court of Protection to appoint a person to act as receiver for the patient. This application is usually made by a near relative who may also be the person seeking to be appointed to act. On the appointment of a receiver the banker should stop the customer's account, inspect the authority of the receiver and open a new account in the name of the receiver. However, where a customer voluntarily enters a hospital for mental treatment this is not in itself sufficient justification for the banker stopping the account and paying over the balance, and the bank was quite wrong to transfer the balance of Rose Burton's account into the name of her husband without suitable authority on the above lines. Having said this, however, the bank should not accept immediately what the solicitors are saying, and certainly insofar as the funds were used to settle hospital fees etc. and other necessary items for Rose Burton, the bank should be in a fairly strong position. The cheques which were drawn on the new account in Ronald Burton's name should therefore be inspected to see what the funds had been used for. In *Scarth v. National Provincial Bank* (1930) the bank successfully defended a claim where funds had been used to pay the patients debts and a similar equitable principle applied in *Liggett (Liverpool) Ltd. v. Barclays Bank Ltd* (1938). Similarly again, in *Beavan, Davis, Banks & Co. v. Beavan* (1912) it was held that cheques drawn for necessities were good, although the bank could not recover its own charges.

In view of the fairly modest sums involved here, a practical solution should be sought and an amicable settlement aimed for. The bank should reply to the solicitor's letter, seeking further information and should interview Ronald Burton. When responding to the solicitors the bank could advise them of the cheques and amounts (presuming some were) paid clearly for the benefit of Rose Burton and could indicate that such payments should stand up if challenged based upon the cases mentioned earlier.

Answer 17

(a) (i) ● Brunners Ltd. is very likely trading *ultra vires*: objects clause in memorandum as formerly builder whereas company now a hotel business.
● If so, lending unrecoverable — security void.
● Relevant case law is *Introductions Ltd. v. National Provincial Bank Ltd.* (1969).
● Reliance on Section 9 European Communities Act 1972 not recommended.

(ii) Directors' borrowing powers limited to amount of issued capital (£50,000): present position therefore *ultra vires* the directors.

● Banks do not rely on exclusion clauses such as:
"temporary loans from company's bankers"
"no longer shall be concerned to see limit is observed".
(Article 79 Table A — Companies Act 1948).
● Calculation:
Bank Overdraft	£20,000
Directors Loan	£34,000
Guarantee for White Ltd.	£20,000
	£74,000

SECTION 3: ANSWERS

- Reliance on Turquand's Case or Section 9 European Communities Act 1972 not recommended.

(b) (i) Company to amend objects clause in memorandum by special resolution in general meeting.

- Write to secretary and have this put in hand immediately, if not already done.
- Certified company resolution to be exhibited to the bank.
- Retrospective effect not possible.
- Clayton's Case will help bank in the meantime as lending becomes "fresh".

(ii) Company to amend articles by special resolution in general meeting to give adequate borrowing powers e.g. £80,000 or unlimited.

- Or special resolution covering directors' powers for overdraft and guarantee.
- Retrospective effect possible, with ratification by ordinary resolution.
- Capitalise reserves or profit and loss account balance.

All the above may not be possible while *ultra vires* company position exists: *Grant v. UN Switchback Railways Co.* (1888).

Answer 18

By S.319 of the Companies Act 1948 (now S. 614 of the 1985 Act) certain payments have priority in a winding-up over all other debts, and these payments include wages or salary of any clerk, servant, workman or labourer during the 4 months preceding the commencement of the winding-up, subject to a maximum of £800 per person. (The amount was increased from £200 by the Insolvency Act 1976.) The Section also allows anyone who has advanced money to a company to pay such wages or salaries to have priority to the extent to which those preferential claims have been satisfied from the advance.

Thus, a bank can nurse a company in low water in so far as it can claim preference (even over a floating charge) for advances for wages and salaries. The inspector has this preference in mind when he suggests opening a separate "Wages and Salaries Account" for the company. Such a separate account is normal banking practice, though it is not legally necessary: *In Re Primrose (Builders) Ltd.* (1950), which has been followed in another wages account case, *In Re Rampgill Mill Ltd.* (1967). It is, however, advisable, because a separate account makes the wages' advances easily ascertainable, and also prevents the operation of the Rule in Clayton's Case (1816) which in a large and active account may mean that credits paid in would wipe out withdrawals for wages and salaries before they were out of time under S.319. Where a bank opened a separate wages account, but incorrectly operated it, nevertheless the bank was able to establish most of its preferential claim, though because of the rule in Clayton's Case the first five items were lost: *In Re James R. Rutherford & Sons Ltd.* (1964). The bank of course, remains an unsecured creditor for any wages and salaries advances which have lost their preferential nature.

The bank must ensure as far as possible that the conditions of S.319 are fulfilled. Only wages and salaries are preferential and any withdrawals not representing these — e.g. Petty Cash — would be rejected by a liquidator as not ranking preferentially. Sometimes banks require to be furnished by the company with a schedule of employees and details of their wages/salaries and confirmation that these persons have been paid these amounts.

Whatever amounts for wages and salaries in the overdrawn account still have preference (i.e. are within S.319 as to time and amount, and are not barred by the Rule in Clayton's Case) should be transferred to the new Wages and Salaries Account. Each week when a new debit is passed for that week's wages and salaries the earliest debit, which will now have lost its priority, can be cleared by a credit from the general account, so that the debit balance on the Wages and Salaries Account will reflect the total of the preferential claim at any given time and nothing else.

If any other accounts have credit balances, then care is needed to ensure that the bank's preferential claim is not reduced by this credit balance being offset against the debit balance on wages account, rather than against other overdrawn balances: *Re E.J. Morel Ltd* (1934).

It should be remembered that a wages claim ranks equally with other preferential creditors and there is no guarantee that in a liquidation, the preferential creditors will be paid in full. Nevertheless, in practice a bank can often help a company in difficulty and derive some comfort from knowing that advances for wages will rank before unsecured creditors and floating charge holders.

Answer 19

The following steps cover the action needed by the bank:

(1)
- The company had called a meeting and intended to go into creditors' voluntarily liquidation, which would commence when the resolutions were passed (Section 280 Companies Act 1948 — Section 588 Companies Act 1985).
- In a creditors' voluntary liquidation there is no "relation back" to the time of the notice, and it would have been permissible to allow the accounts to continue until the resolutions were passed;
- If that action were taken, clearly the branch would monitor the account carefully to ensure that any transactions were normal.
- The transfer to the loan account could therefore have been made on the due date if sufficient funds were present in the current account, and clearly the branch would not have wished to let that current account go overdrawn.
- (The question arises of whether or not the account should be stopped upon receipt of notice and the borrowing called in. The practice here can vary from bank to bank but the terms of the loan agreement should be considered in the context of demanding repayment, particularly since the loan repayments are up to date. The loan can only be called in prior to liquidation if stated to be repayable on demand or if an event of default has occurred which entitles the bank to demand repayment (*Williams & Glyn's Bank Ltd v. Barnes* (1979)).

(2) Upon the passing of resolutions to wind up the company the following applies:

- Upon commencement of the liquidation the accounts need to be stopped and a net figure with interest to date calculated which will be the bank's claim.
- The bank will have no claim for preferential treatment by way of a wages claim if the current account had been kept in credit after receipt of the notices.
- The bank, in order to protect its position, should advise the liquidator of the balances, of the bank's right of set off and the security held. The bank would need to consider whether to ask the liquidator if he will sell the property and account to the bank for the proceeds or whether to sell the property as mortgagees and apply the proceeds in reduction or repayment of the debt.
- The guarantee needs to be called in and any funds received should be credited

to a separate suspense account so that the bank can claim for its full direct debt in the liquidation pending overall clarification of the likely outcome.

Answer 20

A point to be picked up and queried at the outset is whether or not the proposed transactions could possibly constitute an infringement of Sections 42–44 of the Companies Act 1981 which amended the law concerning the giving of financial assistance by a company for the acquisition of its own shares (formerly Section 54 of the 1948 Act applied). In *Belmont Finance Corporation v. William Furniture Ltd.* (1979) it was held that the transfer of assets by a new subsidiary to its parent at less than their true value was an infringement of this section of the Companies Act. The bank should therefore probe this angle and, if necessary, seek legal advice. (The above statutory provisions are now consolidated into Sections 151–158 of the Companies Act 1985.)

The security re-arrangements should be as follows:

Z Ltd. — This company is required to give three unlimited all-monies guarantees for the liabilities of A Ltd, B Ltd and C Ltd in accordance with its Memorandum and Articles of Association. The Memorandum must give specific power to give guarantees. Commercial justification should not pose a problem in view of the overall group trading relationship. The company also needs to execute a debenture giving the usual fixed and floating charge. However, since Z Ltd. is to factor its debts, the bank will need to agree a letter of priority with the factors and be satisfied with the terms of the letter it gives.

A Ltd. — The main company office and factory premises were in the name of this company but are being transferred to B Ltd. The deeds should therefore be released to the company's solicitors on undertaking and when conveyed into B Ltd. should be re-charged to the bank by way of second mortgage, behind the first mortgage being taken by the merchant bank. A priority letter in favour of the merchant bank would be a satisfactory way of dealing with the prior charge. The holding company needs to give a guarantee for the liabilities of the new company Z Ltd. in accordance with its Memorandum and Articles.

B Ltd. and C Ltd. — Both companies need to give all-monies guarantees for the liabilities of Z Ltd., and B Ltd., as mentioned earlier, should give a second mortgage over the factory/office on the bank's usual form. Similarly, a first charge needs to be given over the property formerly belonging to Z Ltd

As C Ltd. is to factor its debts, a letter of priority in favour of the factors needs to be agreed and given in the same way as such a letter of priority is being given by Z Ltd (see earlier).

The above actions should put the bank in the position it requires *vis-à-vis* security.

Answer 21

(i) This advertisement in the London Gazette is the one required by Rule 28 of the Companies (Winding-up) Rules 1949 and is notice to the general public that a petition has been presented by Y Ltd., a creditor, to the High Court for the compulsory winding-up of X Ltd. Details are given as to where and when the court will hear the petition. Presentation of a petition is equivalent to an act of bankruptcy by a person. The date on which the petition was presented is important because if and when the court makes a winding-up order, this is the date from which the winding-up commences, unless there has been a previous resolution for voluntary winding-up — Section 229 of the Companies Act 1948 (now Section 524 of the Companies Act 1985).

At the hearing the court will receive the evidence of Y Ltd., the petitioning creditor, and (if any be offered) that of X Ltd., and other creditors and/or contributaries whether in support of, or opposed to, the petition. The Court will then either make a winding-up order, or dismiss the petition, or sometimes adjourn the hearing to a later date.

The presentation of the petition does not terminate the powers of the directors who continue to run the company until a winding-up order is made and a liquidator appointed (or the petition is dismissed.) The question, however, of what cheques should be paid in the period between the presentation of the petition and its hearing, is a real problem for bankers although to a very large extent, their attitude has had to harden as a result of case law and fairly recent judgements. Section 227 of the Companies Act 1948 (Section 522 of the 1985 Act) states that any disposition of the Company's property after the commencement of the winding-up is void, unless the court orders otherwise, and, as stated above, the winding-up order if made will date back to the presentation of the petition. Bankers were until recently willing generally to take the view that they could safely pay out a credit balance to officials of the company on the grounds that payment to a company of a debt owing to it was not a "disposition" — *Mersey Steel and Iron Co. v. Taylor* (1884).

Cheques payable to third parties were always treated with the utmost caution, although often banks would pay third party cheques which clearly seemed for the benefit of the company and its survival, on the basis that by and large, a liquidator or court would subsequently sanction the payments as having been made for the benefit of the company and its creditors. However, in *Re Grays Inn Construction Co. Ltd.* (1980), the judgement highlighted the problems banks face, and the decision emphasises the extent to which a bank is at risk regarding any transactions on a company customer's account when a winding-up petition has been presented. The decision basically states that any payments into or out of the company's account could be recovered by a liquidator unless made under a court order. Nowadays, therefore, most banks will not permit *any* transactions on an account after notice of presentation of a winding-up petition, and the only safe course the banker can adopt is to pay out only on the production of a court order. In practice, the court will move very quickly if the company's solicitors (or their London agents) make the court aware of the dire urgency attached to the matter of their approving transactions on the bank account.

Therefore the bank here will take a positive stance and make it clear to the company that if any cheques are to be paid, even for wages, the company through its solicitors first must get a court order approving the payments. The bank should help the company as much as possible in trying to get the matter put before the court; failing this the bank should certainly return cheques to the Water Board and M. Cash Ltd. with the answer "winding-up petition presented". As regards the wages cheque, the bank is not really in a better position, but may decide to pay the wages cheque and hope that the Court (or eventually the liquidator) retrospectively approve their action. The fact that a wages advance normally would rank preferentially in a winding-up (Section 319) is not really the point at issue here; what is concerned is whether or not the withdrawal legally will be set aside (or the chances of this happening) if a liquidator subsequently challenges the transaction.

Answer 22

The general rule is that either or any party to a joint account can countermand payment but that the removal of a stop instruction should be made by both parties. Practice on this point can vary from bank to bank but certainly in circumstances such as these, where there is a matrimonial dispute, the greatest care is needed to safeguard as far as is possible against any risk of criticism or a claim being made by one of the parties. The bank should seek an early interview with Mr. & Mrs. Charles and inform them of the bank's requirement regarding the conduct of the account which basically should be that until the dispute is settled, the bank will pay cheques and permit withdrawals only on their joint signatures. The bank should urge them to settle their differences as soon as possible but must not allow the bank to be involved in or dragged into the dispute and as far as the bank is concerned the matter of who had provided the funds now in the account is not relevant. Should they not be able to resolve quickly their dispute and therefore ask to operate separate accounts, the bank could do this, with any transfers from the joint account being authorised by both of them. Care would also be needed as regards any items in the future for paying in, and very careful instruction would be required for such applications of credits.

Answer 23

(a) (i) *Death of a party to a joint account which is in credit.*

On receiving notice of the death of a party to a joint account a banker should return any cheques signed by the deceased alone under authority. If cheques signed by the survivor(s) in accordance with the mandate held are presented, they could *technically speaking*, be returned, for any such mandate is revoked by the death of one of the parties thereto. However, *in practice*, as normally the survivor is free to deal with the balance, cheques so signed could safely be paid and, where necessary, confirmation obtained thereafter. Formal proof of death (e.g. a death certificate) should be exhibited. The banker is not concerned with the claim of the representatives with regard to the balance of the account; they should be referred to the survivor(s). Nor is the banker concerned as to the portion of the balance which must be returned as part of the deceased's estate for duty purposes, but it should be remembered that the Inland Revenue Authorities ask all bankers to remind the representatives of a deceased party to a joint account to mention the account in their returns.

If the account is in debit the banker's position depends on the terms of the mandate. If joint liability only is established, the banker has no claim on the deceased party's estate. If, however, as is the custom, joint and several liability has been established the banker should immediately stop the account to prevent the Rule in Clayton's Case operating to the Bank's detriment, and so preserve his rights against the deceased's estate. Any cheques presented which were drawn by the deceased should be returned and a new account opened for the survivor(s).

(b) (i) *Notice of a Receiving Order against a party to a joint account which is in credit.*

In the event of the banker being notified of the making of a Receiving Order against a party to a joint account which is in credit, the only safe course the banker can adopt is to stop the account pending the *joint* instructions of the solvent party or parties *and* the trustee in bankruptcy. Cheques presented after receipt of notice should be returned, care being taken not to damage the credit of the solvent party or parties in the answer made.

If the account is in debit the banker's position will again depend on whether *joint* liability or *joint and several* liability has been established. In either event the account will be stopped and cheques returned, but if joint liability only has been established, the bankruptcy of one party will discharge his estate. If *joint and several* liability has been established, as is the custom, however, the banker may prove against the bankrupt's estate without prejudice to his rights against the surviving parties. The stopping of the account, of course, will prevent the Rule in Clayton's Case operating to the bank's detriment.

(a)(ii) *Death of a partner in a partnership account which is in credit.*

The death of a partner dissolves the partnership and automatically revokes any mandate for signing on the account. The banker could, therefore, return any cheques presented after the death — whether signed by the deceased partner OR the survivor(s) marked "partner deceased". The surviving partners have, however, power to bind the partnership *for the purpose of winding it up* and in practice, with a credit account, it is customary to pay the firm's cheques presented after the death of a partner, getting the confirmation of the surviving partner(s) if deemed desirable. Here again, the banker is under no duty to account to representatives of the deceased for his share of the partnership assets. In *Backhouse v. Charlton* (1878) it was held that where a banker has no notice of the state of accounts between the deceased partner and the survivor(s), he was under no duty to enquire.

Where the partnership account is in debit, any action by the banker will depend on the nature of the security lodged. If it was the deceased's property, charged by him, or if the banker wished to retain a hold on the private estate of the deceased, the account must be stopped to prevent the Rule in Clayton's Case operating against the bank. Note that, with a Partnership, the Bank's claim against the private Estate of the deceased ranks after that of his private creditors, unless the deceased had joined in a joint and several mandate, in which case the Bank's claim ranks pari passu with the private creditors. If the security held is *partnership* property and sufficient to cover the debt, the account may be continued unbroken for the time being for, here again, the partners surviving are entitled to wind up the partnership business.

(b)(ii) *Partnership account in credit when Receiving Order is made against a partner.*

The bankruptcy of a partner likewise dissolves the partnership, but here too, the surviving partners have power to continue the business for the purpose of winding it up, to get in the assets, and to complete unfinished transactions. Neither the insolvent partner *nor* the Trustee in Bankruptcy has any power to deal with the partnership affairs. If, therefore, there is a credit balance on the partnership account, cheques, other than those signed by the partner against whom a Receiving Order has been made, can be paid and the balance safely released to the solvent partners. It is their responsibility to account to the Trustee for the bankrupt's share of the assets. If cheques signed by the insolvent partner are presented they should not be paid without the confirmation of the solvent partners.

If the partnership account is in debit and the bank requires to retain any rights against the bankrupt's estate, the account must be broken. If joint and several liability has not been established, the bank will be postponed in proving on the bankrupt partner's private estate until all his separate creditors have been paid in

SECTION 3: ANSWERS

full. If, however, joint and several liability *has* been established, the banker can prove as a creditor on equal footing with the private creditors. The importance of stipulating for joint and several liability is, therefore, readily appreciated.

Answer 24

Although there is nothing to suggest that the account has not been conducted in a satisfactory manner since it was opened, Mr. Ruddle's request to continue it on the existing basis, without Mr. Gilbert's name needs careful consideration. If the bank agrees to Mr. Ruddle's request and allows the account to continue on that basis, then the Rule in Clayton's Case (*Devaynes v. Noble* (1816)) will begin to operate against the bank so far as it is relying on Mr. Gilbert's estate to clear the indebtedness, since all credits received will reduce the estate's liability. Furthermore any cheques drawn by Mr. Ruddle will create fresh borrowing in respect of which Mr. Gilbert's estate will not be liable. Therefore if the bank wishes to preserve the liability of Mr. Gilbert's estate for the overdraft, the account must be stopped. A new account can be opened for Mr. Ruddle in his sole name. As Mr. Ruddle wishes to retain a borrowing limit of £1500 the bank needs to look at this request as an entirely fresh proposition and to assess it accordingly, deciding whether or not security is needed. Additionally, the bank will need to consider if Mr. Ruddle is financially able to carry on the business himself, since to do this he will need to buy out the interest of Mr. Gilbert's estate in the business. Possibly, this will mean that Mr. Ruddle may have to consider finding a new partner who will provide some incoming capital which can go towards assisting in the purchase of Mr. Gilbert's estate's interest.

The bank should see and assess recent audited figures for the business to ascertain whether the business is in good health; if any more recent financial information can be produced — perhaps management figures, budgets etc. — these should aid the assessment. The figures also will indicate Mr. Ruddle's own position financially and his potential for servicing the borrowings from the bank, should the bank agree to allow him the facility he is asking for.

Answer 25

(a) The bank's existing mandate authorises the bank to pay cheques signed by any one partner but clearly two of the partners for some reason wish to change this instruction. In view of the letter received from Hall and Green, the safest course for the bank is to advise all the three partners that it regards the former mandate as cancelled and that, in the absence of a satisfactory fresh mandate, it will only honour cheques bearing the signatures of all three partners. The bank should not act upon the request made by Hall and Green but should insist to all the partners that they quickly resolve the apparent problem, and inform them that if they do not do this then they may have to make alternative banking arrangements. Care must be taken with the answer on any cheques returned pending the mandate being resolved, and an appropriate answer would be "Cheque not drawn in accordance with mandate".

In practice if the bank adopts this stance, it will very likely bring it home to the partners, in particular Hall and Green, that the bank is not prepared to be dragged into any partner disputes and that the funds in the partnership account will only be released against the discharge of all the partners.

(b) Here the bank has clearly disobeyed its mandate and is therefore prima facie liable for the amounts debited in contravention of the mandate. However, the question arises as to whom the bank is liable and to what quarter any refund is necessary. If there is a dispute between Jones and Green and if the funds withdrawn by Green have been utilised for non-partnership debts, then clearly the bank will have to reimburse Jones, or more accurately repay the monies to the partnership. However, if the bank can show that the cheques it paid on one signature did in fact settle genuine partnership debts then, in the absence of other factors, its position may not be so serious. The bank may be able to gain comfort by way of subrogation — *Liggett (Liverpool) Ltd. v. Barclays Bank Ltd.* (1928).

In the question set, the bank will need to ascertain what the relationship is between the two partners and what lies behind Jones' revealing this matter, in order to form any real view as to whether the bank's having disobeyed the mandate is likely to have serious consequences.

Section 4

Answers

Answer 26

If the three executors wish to open an Executors' account and to borrow for the purpose of paying capital transfer tax, the following are the issues arising:

- Examine the will to confirm names of executors.
- Obtain specimen signatures, addresses and other details obtained when opening a new current account.
- Have standard bank mandate for Executors completed, establishing joint and several liability and incorporating their undertaking to prove the will and repay advance out of the first monies received from the estate.
- Obtain details of deceased's estate: total value: assessment of C.T.T. payable: breakdown of assets will indicate the source of early repayment of the bank borrowing (i.e. from liquid assets in the estate).
- Remember that securities deposited by deceased will not secure this borrowing: *Farhael v. Farhael* (1871).
- Executors have power to pledge deceased's assets, but is only valid after Probate (thus lending to pay C.T.T. is essentially unsecured).
- In practice, a turn (say 2%) taken over and above the deceased's credit balances (if any) rather than allowing full set-off interest.

If customer died intestate, advance could be made to widow as next of kin, but following should be noted:

- Account would be her sole responsibility and designated "Administratrix a/c" instead of "Executors' a/c."
- No mandate needed, but specimen signature and other details to be obtained.
- No power to pledge deceased's assets as have executors (but not of significance in practice — see above).

Answer 27

The problem here is to weigh up the advantages and disadvantages of the alternative securities offered, and to decide which type of security would be preferable.

As regards the proposed mortgage by the trustees to secure their own account the first point to establish is whether they have express powers under the will to borrow, and, if they have not, whether the borrowing is within the scope of S.16 of the Trustee Act 1925. This Section provides that where trustees are authorised by the instrument, if any, creating the trust or by law to pay or apply capital money subject to the trust for any purpose in any manner, they shall have power to mortgage all or any part of the trust property.

The banker would normally take legal advice on a matter such as this and indeed it could well be that the mortgage document to be executed by the trustees will need to be drawn up specially as the bank standard form of legal charge may not be completely appropriate. When advising on the trustees' power to borrow, the legal adviser could at the same time be asked if a specially drawn up charge document is needed or not.

If both trustees duly mortgage the property as proposed to secure their own account, the bank will have all the rights and remedies of a mortgagee against the property, including foreclosure.

The alternative is to take as security a mortgage by the beneficiary, Ann, of her equitable interest in the trust property, for she is over 18, but it must first be established whether her interest is absolute or contingent. If it is the latter, so that her interest may be destroyed in certain eventualities, e.g. by her pre-deceasing her mother, it will be necessary to effect an appropriate life policy as cover against these possibilities. Mortgages of reversion are occasionally taken by banks, the form of charge being specially prepared by the bank's solicitors. Written notice of such a charge must be given to the trustees to determine priority, and their acknowledgement obtained, together with a confirmation that no notices of prior charges are outstanding. As this is a mortgage of personalty (not realty) the bank will have no right to foreclosure but merely the right to sell the reversion.

In the particular circumstances set out in the question it would probably be preferable to make the loan direct to Ann and take the suggested security from her, for she is to enjoy the benefit of the advance and it is to her that the bank will in reality be looking for interest and repayment. However, either method could be acceptable to the bank and therefore the bank would be happy to structure the facility in accordance with the method preferred by the parties concerned.

Answer 28

The coins could not be handed over by the bank until probate has been obtained, for executor(s) are not entitled to withdraw articles deposited with the bank until probate of the will can be exhibited to the bank. However, as the value of the coins will have to be ascertained for their inclusion in the deceased's assets in the application for probate, P. Talbot should be told that the bank would have no objection to a professional valuer attending at the branch to inspect the coins and make a valuation of them. This will be done under strict supervision of branch officials.

Alternatively — and exceptionally — the coin collection could be released to the solicitors acting for the estate (if they were not already well known to the branch, a good report should be obtained) against their undertaking to hold the collection to the bank's order until production of probate together with a discharge from the executor. This course would mean making an inventory of the coins (which would involve assessing their grade or condition) and being much more difficult than having the valuer call, it would not be encouraged.

SECTION 4: ANSWERS

Answer 29

The bank should ask to see a death certificate for Mr. Horne and should enter the details of this appropriately in the bank's records. The accounts of James Horne should be stopped and any cheques presented would need to be returned unpaid with the answer "Drawer deceased." Interest on the deposit account should be calculated and applied up to the date of death.

The bank should satisfy itself as to the identity of Mrs. Horne (unless she is known to the branch) and her standing, and a status report could be obtained from the branch at which she banks. The bank would not insist upon letters of administration being obtained if the estate is small and most banks have their own figure within their own procedures as being the maximum balance they will release without insisting on probate or letters of administration. The Administration of Estates (Small Payments) Act 1965, as subsequently amended, covers this sort of situation also. The bank would take an indemnity from Mrs. Horne, indemnifying them against loss etc. should someone else subsequently take out letters of administration or probate (if a will came to light) and prove a better right to the deceased's balances. (Should there be other close members of the family, the bank may have these join in the indemnity also.)

Answer 30

Although the manager will naturally wish to be as helpful as possible to Mrs. Bondim, his prime concern must be to safeguard the position of the bank. If Mr. Bondim has died intestate, then the position of Mrs. Bondim may turn out to be a difficult one. It is possible that she has acquired some right to the estate of Mr. Bondim through her relationship with him but this is not certain, and she would be well-advised to seek legal advice of her own from a solicitor, who should be able to help her in this direction. The bank will have to stop the accounts of Mr. Bondim. Its lending is well secured and the bank should therefore be fairly relaxed about its lending exposure as it is hard to imagine that repayment will not be forthcoming from one source or another, unless some defect exists arising out of the way the bank took its security. The bank legally should negotiate terms of repayment with Mr. Bondim's legal representatives , and will therefore need at the present time to keep in touch with the position to establish whether a will has been found and, if so, who are the executors. On the other hand, if Mr. Bondim died intestate, then someone will need to take out letters of administration in order to wind up the estate. This again could give rise to disputes and so again it would be advisable for Mrs. Bondim to seek legal advice immediately. Mrs. Bondim will have to resolve her own problems in respect of the delicatessen where she wishes to continue to trade. Unless a will comes to light in which she participates sufficiently to be able to do so, then the business could pass to relatives. She is in a difficult position, the more so because the bank will not be able to make available to her the current account balance which now rests in the names of the executors or administrators for the time being and may, in the long run, turn out to belong to a beneficiary other than Mrs. Bondim. Alternatively, the business may have to be sold.

It would depend on the circumstances as to whether or not the bank felt it might help Mrs. Bondim financially but it seems there is little the bank can do. If the previous days takings are paid in, the bank would have to set them aside for the estate in a suspense account although presumably Mrs. Bondim will hang on to these funds to help her to keep the business going until the situation has been clarified. The business cannot be regarded as her own at the present time and certainly the bank could not permit any transfer from the current account into her name. The bank will need to see the death certificate and eventually letters of administration or probate will need to be furnished so that the bank can properly sort out the balances of Mr. Bondim.

Section 5

Answers

Answer 31

(a) (i) A banker who pays a post-dated cheque before its date is *disobeying his customer's mandate* and will therefore have to stand any loss which results from his actions. (It may, of course, be that the customer has made a genuine mistake and in practice it is often possible to get in touch with him to ascertain his wishes should a post-dated cheque be presented for payment.) There is an added risk too that if a post-dated cheque has been paid and a cheque subsequently presented is returned for lack of funds, the banker may render himself liable for damages in an action for injuring his customer's credit. Moreover, if the banker pays a post-dated cheque to protect his customer and does not debit the cheque but holds it until the due date the customer may fail in the meantime and the banker will be left with the cheque on his hands or the customer may countermand payment before the date of the cheque or he may die or a Garnishee order may be served.

(a) (ii) If a banker pays a "stopped" cheque he will be liable for any loss his customer may sustain. Here too, he may be involved in an action for injuring his customer's credit if, having paid a stopped cheque he later returns another or others for lack of funds. The banker's only remedy if he has paid a stopped cheque and his customer insists on being reimbursed is to claim the actual goods (if any and they can be identified) in respect of which the cheque was issued.

(iii) A banker paying a cheque bearing a forged endorsement may be afforded protection by Section 60 of the Bills of Exchange Act 1882. To claim the protection of Section 60, he must have paid the cheque in good faith and in the ordinary course of business. It should be noted if the cheque is crossed, the provisions of Section 80 must also be observed, and that Section 60, when read in conjunction with Section 80, means that payment in the ordinary course of business means payment to a banker; if crossed specially, to the banker to whom it is crossed. These Sections remain unaffected by the Cheques Act 1957, though this Act has largely dispensed with the endorsement of cheques.

(b) (i) and (ii) Since the Cheques Act 1957 it is immaterial to the collecting banker whether a cheque is uncrossed or crossed. Provided he acts "in good faith and without negligence" and receives payment of a cheque for a customer (or having credited a customer's account with the amount of the cheque receives payment thereof for himself), he is afforded full protection by Section 4 of the Cheques Act 1957, and should his customer's title be void or defective, the banker will incur no liability to the true owner.

In the absence of this statutory protection, he would incur the ordinary common law liability for converting the property of the true owner being in this case the face value of the cheque.

(c) If a banker exchanges a cheque crossed "Not negotiable" he does so entirely at his own risk. If there is no question of defective title, the banker, who is, in effect collecting the cheque for himself may enforce payment against the drawer and other parties but if there is any defect in the title the banker will have no better right than that of the person for whom it was exchanged. (Many banks use a special "Exchange" form for cashing cheques and if cashing the cheque for a customer this form embodies certain safeguards for the banker as it authorises the banker to debit the customer's account if the cheque is unpaid. At law, Exchange Forms may be unnecessary with order cheques, since the endorsement gives authority to debit the account. The danger, of course, is, the customer may insist that he paid the cheque into the account and did not cash it. The Exchange Form will be sufficient evidence against him.)

Answer 32

This question centres round the time factor in the payment of cheques and is similar to the case of *Baines v. National Provincial Bank Ltd.* (1927), in which the Lord Chief Justice held that a cheque paid by a bank five minutes after closing time was paid in the ordinary course of business. Thus, the bank, which here operates both as collecting bank and paying bank, collected and paid the cheque in the ordinary course of business, because there is no need to adhere strictly to the 3.30 deadline (which is fixed by banks for their own convenience, and not by statute as is the case with the hours of business of public houses). In any event, it is banking practice to incorporate sub-branch work in the day's work of the parent branch when the sub-branch clerk has returned. Accordingly, the bank is not liable to Hank because at the time when he attempted to stop payment, the cheque had already been paid in good faith and in the ordinary course of business, for the payee was entitled to present the cheque by the quickest available means. In fact, whilst attempting to be smart, Hank has been caught out by his own inadequate knowledge of the locality's banking premises.

The letter to Hank's solicitor should say that the bank is allowed a reasonable margin of time after the advertised closing time in which to pay cheques, and that, therefore, the cheque was paid in the ordinary course of business.

Answer 33

The situation here concerns two matters; firstly the action needed upon the marriage of a spinster customer and secondly the collection of cheques thereafter with the risk of conversion. The bank should ask to see a copy of Ann Price's marriage certificate or, if that is not now this bank's practice, they should ask her to sign a form stating that she was married and that she is now known as Ann Shepherd. A fresh specimen signature should be obtained and new cheque books ordered in her married name, assuming that she wants the account to be in that name. (She has not said that she wishes anything other than that, saying merely that she will continue to carry out her work under her maiden name.) The most straightforward way is to change the name of her account over to her married name, but to be aware and have on record that she may tender cheques in favour of Ann Price. Although the practical risk may here be small, the question of conversion has to be considered and therefore there is a need to make enquiry as to the cheque payable to Roger Shepherd. There is probably a straightforward explanation which will be forthcoming and if the bank receives this in response to its enquiry, it can proceed with the collection. The registration of business names was abolished by the Companies Act 1981 so that no longer would it be appropriate to ask the customer for sight of the certificate under the Registration of Business Names Act. The question arises of enquiring who Roger Shepherd's employers are (as was shown desirable in *Lloyds Bank Ltd. v. Savory* (1933)) although nowadays some banks do not make such enquiries.

Answer 34

The danger here is that of conversion, as the bank has been collecting cheques payable to one company for the account of another without any enquiries having been made. The protection of S.4 of the Cheques Act 1957 would therefore not be available as the bank would not be able to show that it had acted "without negligence." It has to be remembered that each limited company (even if parent and wholly-owned subsidiary) are separate legal persons in law and the similarity in names and parent/subsidiary relationship are immaterial as far as a collecting banker is concerned. Clearly a tactful approach is called for and perhaps a social meeting could be arranged, perhaps a luncheon, when it could be put to the company that a separate account ought to be opened for the subsidiary. Should it transpire that for some good reason this was not acceptable, if upon further investigation the entire background seemed safe, the bank may regard itself as sufficiently protected in the circumstances by taking Board resolutions from each company authorising the bank to collect cheques in favour of the subsidiary for the account of the holding company and suitably idemnifying the bank if any loss was subsequently suffered by that action. Unless there was a very good reson for not opening an account in the name of the subsidiary, the bank should start out with the intention of having an account opened in the subsidiary's name, into which the cheques payable to that company's name should be credited.

Answer 35

This question implies that the debiting of the collected cheque will cause an overdraft that the payees are unable to meet. If the account is sufficiently in credit to stand the debiting of the returned cheque or if the bank is happy to permit any overdrawn position caused by the return of the cheque, then obviously the bank will not require to submit any claim against the drawer and the matter will have to be dealt with by The Bollin Printing Company.

The bank's position revolves around Section 27(3) and Section 29 of the Bills of Exchange Act 1882. A banker clearly gives value for a cheque if he allows the customer to draw against the cheque in anticipation of the proceeds being received. The banker then has a lien on the cheque to the value of the amount so drawn and by Section 27(3) when a holder of a bill has a lien on it he is deemed to be a holder for value. As a holder for value the banker may sue any parties to the bill but may be defeated by any defect of title of his predecessors. The banker should not part with the cheque for if possession is given up a lien is lost and is not revived by subsequent repossession of the cheque — *Westminster Bank Ltd. v. Zang* (1966). In practice, when a banker has permitted withdrawals in anticipation of a collected cheque being paid and the cheque is returned unpaid, the amount of the cheque is often not debited to the customer's account but to a suspense account in the bank's books to show clearly that the bank has given value.

Answer 36

This question concerns the protection afforded to the collecting banker by S.4 of the Cheques Act, 1957. Like the now repealed S.82 of the Bills of Exchange Act, 1882 which it replaced, S.4 requires, *inter alia*, that the collecting banker should act "without negligence".

It has been held that whilst the words "Account payee only" on a cheque have no statutory significance, a banker collecting a cheque so crossed for someone other than the payee is negligent and loses his statutory protection: *House Property Co. of London Ltd. and Others v. London County and Westminster Bank Ltd.* (1915).

The crossing does not restrict the negotiability of the cheque but puts the collecting banker on enquiry and he does not lose the protection of Section 4 if he makes enquiries and these are reasonably answered: *Bevan v. National Bank Ltd.* (1906) and *Importers Co. v. Westminster Bank Ltd.* (1927).

Therefore, in the question set, the bank (preferably through its own solicitors) should rebut the claim made by Hill's solicitors on the grounds that it made suitable enquiries which were satisfactorily answered as to the bona fides of the transaction and therefore retains its statutory protection. Whether or not this would be so held would depend upon the Court's view of whether the bank acted with sufficient care and, of course, in view of the fairly modest amount involved the bank may well decide to settle with Hill should he press.

Section 6

Answers

Answer 37

(a) Here the bank has taken only an equitable charge by way of a memorandum of deposit signed by Mrs. King over various shares in her name which she has lodged. When the bank seeks eventually to enforce its security, it emerged that she is not the beneficial owner of these shares, but holds them as trustee for her children. Therefore, the prior equitable interest of the children will prevail over the later equitable interest of the bank, for "where the equities are equal, the first in time prevails". Had the bank taken a legal charge over the shares without notice of the prior equity, the bank's legal title would have prevailed, but once the bank learns of the prior equity, it is too late to convert its title from an equitable one to a legal one even if it holds blank transfers. The Bank has no claim against the shares, though Mrs. King of course, remains liable for her indebtedness. If she does not repay, a court action will be necessary and in this event the bank may prefer to get the court's instructions about the shares rather than hand them back to a trustee who has committed a breach of trust.

(b) The reason for not taking partly paid shares into the name of the bank's nominee company is to avoid liability for future calls on the shares if and when they may be made. If the nominee company was the registered holder it would be bound to pay the calls, and by S.212 of the Companies Act 1948 this legal liability may continue, in certain circumstances on the liquidation of the company, for 12 months after the nominee company has ceased to hold them. Partly paid shares may be quite valuable, but for the reason given they are held under an equitable mortgage only, so that the depositor remains the registered owner.

Answer 38

This question concerns the standing of equitable interests as against legal interests and the priority of different equitable interests.

Different equitable interests rank in date order (Maxim "Where the equities are equal, the first in time prevails") but a legal title taken in good faith and without notice of any equitable interest will rank first (Maxim "Where the equities are equal, the law prevails").

An analysis of the various securities held by the bank shows that the bank has an unassailable legal title to the Victory Bonds (which are fully negotiable so that title passes by delivery, thus, in *London Joint Stock Bank v. Simmons* (1892) where a stockbroker had pledged bearer bonds, belonging to his clients, for his own indebtedness, the bank's right to retain the bonds was upheld). The same probably applies in the case of the International Nickel shares in a "marking name" and endorsed. The International Nickel shares in own name are probably not in practice bearer securities.

To the rest of the securities the bank has merely an equitable title — the minor variations in the methods of approach to the individual securities are irrelevant here — and it will have to release them to the claimant. If the dividends are specifically charged by the memorandum of deposit, those on the securities to which the bank has a legal title belong to the bank, and the others to the claimant; if the dividends are not so charged, all must be paid over to the claimant.

The bank should therefore inform the brother of this and, should the securities to which the bank has a legal title not realise sufficient to discharge the borrowing, then the bank will have to seek proposals from the customer's personal representatives.

Answer 39

The assistant manager has acted far too hastily and maybe quite unnecessarily since the suspension of dealings in the shares does not necessarily mean that the shares have lost their value. Frequently shares are suspended by the Stock Exchange at the company's request, when take-over talks are in progress and it is quite possible that dealings might resume, after a short delay, and at a higher price.

In *Buckingham v. Midland Bank* (1895) a branch revalued its security and, due to concern at its lower value, merged the customer's current and loan accounts and returned cheques. In such circumstances the bank leaves itself open to a claim for damages for wrongful dishonour of cheques. The damages could be assessed on the principle in *Gibbons v. Westminster* (1939) which is that the customer must prove special damage unless he is a trader, whereas damage will be presumed if he is. In *Jayson v. Midland Bank Ltd.* (1968) the words "Refer to Drawer" were held to be libellous. Thus the actions of the assistant manager have placed the bank in a difficult position, and the bank should contact the presenting bank as quickly as possible and explain that the cheque was returned in error and that it would be paid on representation. If that bank has contacted their customer, efforts should be made to contact the payee both by telephone and in writing, to explain the error and to assure the payee that the dishonour was no reflection on Mr. Parker's creditworthiness. Mr. Parker himself should obviously be contacted and asked to ignore the letter sent to him yesterday and suitable apologies should be offered.

On the question of the credit balance being set off against Mr. Parker's joint account, then this was incorrect due to the reason behind the action of the assistant manager having been quite ill-founded, although in other and valid circumstances (e.g. bankruptcy) the joint and several liability undertaken by Mr. Parker on the joint account would have enabled the bank to set off the credit balance on Mr. Parker's account against either his loan account, or the joint current account. Relative case law on the topic of set off is *Garnett v. McKewan* (1872), *Greenhalgh v. Union Bank of Manchester* (1924) and *National Westminster v. Halesowen Presswork and Assemblies Ltd.* (1972).

Answer 40

Nowadays the usual form of bank debenture includes both a fixed and floating charge. Property, plant and machinery, and debtors would normally be subject to the fixed charge, with the other assets such as stock and work in progress coming under the floating charge. However, the question states that only a floating charge is to be taken here, which although giving priority over unsecured creditors, does not bind the assets as does a fixed charge — the characteristics of a floating charge were laid down in *Re Yorkshire Woolcombers Association* (1903).

The principal weaknesses of a floating charge as security are as follows:

- A floating charge is often worth least when the holder seeks to rely on it. Assets may have diminished by unprofitable trading, or been realised to meet pressing unsecured creditors, thus reducing the value of the floating charge.
- Certain preferential creditors under S.319 of the Companies Act 1948 rank ahead of the floating charge (e.g. rates and taxes, wages and salaries, subject to certain limitations as to time and amount). (Now Section 614 Companies Act 1985.)
- The company may create fixed charges, legal or equitable, over assets embraced by the floating charge (e.g. book debts which may be the subject of a fixed charge to a factoring company) and these fixed charges will take priority over the floating charge. However, to avoid this situation bank floating charges incorporate an undertaking not to create fixed mortgages or charges ranking ahead of or *pari passu* with the floating charge, but such a restriction will not be any protection unless it is brought to the notice of a subsequent mortgagee. Registration of the floating charge at Companies House under S.95 does not constitute such notice, unless specific reference to the restriction is made on the Companies Form 47 filed in respect of the charge.
- Execution creditors may obtain priority on certain assets before the bank can intervene and, if execution has been levied before a receiver can be appointed under the charge, the execution creditor is entitled to retain the proceeds of his collection. The bank should therefore act speedily once it is clear that the company is getting into financial difficulties.
- Assets may successfully be claimed by their suppliers (usually stocks) if supplied on terms whereby title passes only when the goods are paid for — *Aluminium Industrie Vaassen BV v. Romalpa Aluminium Ltd.* (1976).
- By S.322 a floating charge created within 12 months before the commencement of winding-up shall, unless it is proved that the company was solvent at the time of the creation of the charge, be invalid, except to the amount of any cash paid to the company at the time of, or subsequently to the creation of, and in consideration of the charge. However, the Rule in Clayton's Case (1816), as applied in *Re. Thomas Mortimer Ltd.* (1925) and reaffirmed in *Re Yeovil Glove Co. Ltd.* (1965), here assists the bank as past advances are gradually reduced and finally wiped out by credits lodged and payments out are fresh advances within the charge. Every effort should be taken to see that the maximum turnover is passed through the account and the company kept out of liquidation during the 12 months "hardening period", unless it was ascertained that the company was solvent (i.e. could pay its debts as they fell due) at the time the floating charge was taken.
- The bank also needs to be aware of the danger of any charge it takes being subsequently challenged by a liquidator as a fraudulent preference. Since a fraudulent preference needs to be a *voluntary* preference of a creditor, the bank, if it decides to take the floating charge, should make this an absolute condition of it continuing to provide assistance in order that it is not voluntarily being preferred.

Answer 41

By S.322(1) of the Companies Act 1948 (since consolidated into S.617 of the Companies Act 1985) "where a company is being wound up a floating charge on the property or undertaking of the company created within 12 months of the commencement of the winding-up shall, unless it is proved that the company immediately after the creation of the charge was solvent, be invalid except to the amount of any cash paid to the company at the time of or subsequent to the creation of, and in consideration for, the charge."

It follows that as the Wilkman Trading Co. Ltd., went into liquidation on 3rd August, seven months after the creation of the floating charge in favour of West Bank Ltd., on 3rd January, (i.e. within the "hardening" period of the charge) the floating charge is invalid in respect of the *overdraft* of £16,000 existing on 3rd January, unless the company was solvent at that date. The *fixed* charge forming the security for the loan of £20,000, however, remains good.

This is an instance where the Rule in Clayton's Case, as applied in *Re Thomas Mortimer Ltd.* (1925) and *Re Yeovil Glove Co. Ltd.* (1965) would assist the bank so that assuming that the company was not solvent on 3rd January, the bank's position is as follows:

    LOAN   £20,000   OVERDRAFT   £19,000

(a) The Loan is secured by the fixed charge;

(b) During the seven months "hardening" period of the floating charge £12,000 has been paid into the current account, so, by the application of the Rule in Clayton's Case, reducing the original debt of £16,000 outstanding on 3rd January to £4,000. This £4,000 is unsecured, as the floating charge is invalid in respect of the debt outstanding at the date of the creation of the charge.

(c) During the same period £15,000 has been advanced to the company by way of further overdraft and since this £15,000 was lent *subsequent to the creation of the floating charge*, it is secured thereby. Assuming that there are sufficient floating assets to cover the charge, the bank's loss would be £4,000 less any dividend which may be received from the liquidation should there be any surplus assets. If the company was solvent on 3rd January, i.e. when the floating charge was created, the whole current account overdraft would be secured by it. It must be noted that preferential creditors take priority over the floating charge, but not over the fixed charge.

Answer 42

As regards the deeds and the assignment of the contract moneys, the bank is in the unhappy position of having no security, because neither charge was registered with the Registrar of Companies within 21 days of its creation as required by S.95 of the Companies Act 1948, and in consequence they are void as against the liquidator and creditors of the company, but the debt holds good and becomes immediately repayable. Thus the bank becomes an unsecured creditor, and on the appointment of a liquidator it will have to hand back the title deeds to him. The liquidator will also be entitled to receive any amounts paid after his appointment in respect of the contract. (The registration section is now S.395 of the Companies Act 1985.)

To elaborate a little on the question of registration under the Act, the mere deposit of deeds with intention to charge creates an equitable mortgage, which must be registered as a charge on land. The facts regarding the charge on the contract moneys resemble those in *Re Kent and Sussex Sawmill Ltd.* (1946), so that the effect of the authority given by the Company to the Corporation (particularly in view of the reference to irrevocability) is to constitute a charge on book debts which must be registered.

However, the actual position of the bank may not be too bad, depending on how far the managing director's forecast is fulfilled. If the directors of the company, within the five weeks preceding the date of the passing of the winding-up resolution, make a declaration of solvency, i.e. declare that the company will be able to pay its debts in full within 12 months, and file this declaration with the Registrar before that date, the winding-up will be a members' voluntary winding-up. The bank can then reasonably expect the debt to be discharged in full within 12 months. Should it prove impossible to make the declaration of solvency, the winding-up will be a creditors' voluntary winding-up, and the bank will be unlikely to receive payment in full but only a dividend.

Whichever type of voluntary winding-up it proves to be, the bank need not stop the company's accounts until the resolution is passed, as that is the commencement of the winding up. The company in general meeting will then appoint a liquidator, whereupon the powers of the directors cease except insofar as specially sanctioned.

Answer 43

The legal position as to the subsequent dating and registration of an originally undated charge by a company is complicated. In *Esberger & Son Ltd. v. Capital and Counties Bank* (1913) the bank took an undated but otherwise completed memorandum of deposit of title deeds from the company in 1910, held it unregistered until 14th June 1911, when the manager dated it that date and registered it on 3rd July 1911. The charge was set aside on the ground that the time when the charge was actually executed was the operative day, not the date it bore, and so registration was well outside the 21 day period. However, S.98(2) of the Companies Act 1948 provides that the Registrar's certificate of registration of the mortgage or charge shall be conclusive evidence that the requirements of the Act as to registration have been complied with. In *National Provincial and Union Bank of England v. Charnley* (1924) the Court of Appeal considered a similar provision in the Companies Act 1908 and refused to go behind the Registrar's certificate and upheld the charge even though the subject-matter of the charge was wrongly described. Again, in *Re Eric Holmes (Property) Ltd.* (1965) a charge incorrectly dated was upheld, the judge distinguishing Esberger's Case and relying on Charnley's Case and S.98(2). In *Re. C.L. Nye ltd.* (1970), where a charge had been dated some months after execution and registered within 21 days of the date it bore, the Court of Appeal followed its own decision in Charnley's Case and held that the charge was valid.

Bank securities ought to be legally watertight, and not likely to involve expensive litigation — the House of Lords could take a different view of the matter. In these circumstances, the proposed method of taking the floating charge should be politely declined; the bank's reply could confirm that the bank is willing to make the advance against a properly sealed and dated floating charge, if and when the company finds it necessary to take bank borrowing, the charge being registered within 21 days at the Companies Registry. It would be mentioned that as regards the registration of the charge (which will be publicised in commercial gazettes and so on) having an adverse effect on the company's standing, the directors are perhaps over-apprehensive about this, bearing in mind the great number of charges nowadays effected by companies as a whole. Indeed the banker should point out to the directors that the giving of a floating charge and the registration of this could be viewed as a sign of the company's strength, not its weakness, on the grounds that it implies that the bank is willing to lend directly against the company's own assets.

Section 7

Answers

Answer 44

The question specifies leasehold "deeds", so the land is unregistered, and the features of a lease as regards its acceptability as security and the procedure whereby it is charged are as follows:

The value of the lease will usually fall as its term diminishes. Therefore, if reductions are not made in borrowing, the value of the security could be less than the outstanding debt.

Examination of the lease — probably with the aid of branch solicitors — for any onerous provisions:

> Can the lease be assigned?
> To what extent is the tenant liable for repairs and decorating?
> Forfeiture clauses, e.g. if rent not paid?
> Any special restrictions on user of the premises?

Has Holmes had a professional valuation undertaken of the lease? If so, this will throw light on what value can perhaps be placed on the lease quite independently from the goodwill element attached to the business?

Over and above, any views expressed by the valuer, what is the bank's view of the property which is leased? Would it be at all realisable? i.e. would there be any demand for a short term lease of that property, bearing in mind its location, site, nature etc. should Holmes fail in his venture?

The original lease and any assignments must be lodged to form a complete chain of title.

Searches must be made in the Land Charges Register and also in the Local Land Charges Registers.

The bank's form of legal mortgage must be completed and then executed by the customer.

Notice of the bank's charge must be given to the lessor if this is required under the lease.

It must be ascertained that adequate insurance of the premises is in force, and the bank's interest notified to the insurers.

Answer 45

The security available to the bank under the arrangement proposed is in the form of a sub-mortgage i.e. a charge over the mortgage given in favour of Mr. Morgan by the company. A vital factor to be aware of when taking this type of security is that the bank's sub-charge can only be as good as the charge by the company to Mr. Morgan and therefore, the latter will need careful investigation before it can be accepted that a sub-mortgage will provide good security for the bank. Since the question refers to a charge certificate, the land involved here is clearly registered land.

The following steps will be necessary:

(The bank's security is to be a sub-mortgage by Leonard Morgan. The bank's security cannot be better than his — therefore his title and the amount outstanding are of paramount importance).

(a) Check the charge by the company to Morgan (registered land)
- mortgage (inside the charge certificate) sealed by company in accordance with company's memorandum and articles.
- *Intra vires* the company's and directors' powers (borrowing — charging — quorum).
- Registered at Companies Registration Office within 21 days of creation (Section 95 Companies Act 1948 — now S.395 of the 1985 Act)
- Company search to ensure no prior charge.
- Check title held: e.g. absolute; good leasehold.
- Check for adequate insurance; has notice to fire company been given?
- Terms of charge to Morgan, bank's rights no better.
- Repayment arrangements; amount now outstanding?
- Valuation; professional? Adequate for purposes?
- Local searches; satisfactory?
- Obtain opinion that company is good for its repayment instalments.

(b) Sub-mortgage by Leonard Morgan.
- Morgan to execute bank's standard form of sub-mortgage.
- Bank forwards this, copy and charge certificate to Land Registry and receives certificate of sub-charge in exchange.
- Bank gives notice to company; asks how much is outstanding and requests confirmation that future payments will come direct to bank.
- Bank write down value of its security upon each payment.
- Bank gives notice to insurance company and obtains acknowledgement.

Answer 46

This question asks if any *special* problems are likely to be encountered, and therefore it is not necessary to go into the formalities relating to the taking of a second charge which is a common form of banking security nowadays.

Two difficulties arise; both being related to the fact that the land is registered. The first is that, as the first mortgagee holds only an equitable charge as far as the Land Register is concerned (since he only lodged Notice of Deposit); it is not possible for the bank to be given the legal charge it is asking for. Section 64 of the Land Registration Act makes it necessary for the Land Certificate to be produced to the Land Registry on each occasion that there is a disposition of the property and, in law, the creation of a legal charge is regarded as a disposition. As Mr. Dodds has the Land Certificate, the bank will not be able to register its charge. It is therefore necessary to seek the aid of Mr. Dodds whereby he lodges the Land Certificate at the Land Registry, and obtains a legal charge in the form of a charge certificate. However, Land Registry fees would be involved and these are costly which means that Mr. Dodds may well not be willing to co-operate with the bank in this way, particularly since he was apparently quite happy with his equitable first mortgage. In this event, the bank might offer to pay the fees but, if it does so, will no doubt obtain reimbursement from the customer in the overall security charge it applies for the transaction.

If the first charge is not registered because of lack of co-operation, the bank could lodge a caution, which means that if there are any attempts subsequently to deal in the land, the bank will be notified. This is however not a very satisfactory position to be in.

The second difficulty, is due to the property being domestic property which means that if there are any other occupants, such as Mrs. Mosley, she might have an overriding interest under Section 70 of the Land Registration Act 1925 which would rank ahead of the bank. To obtain a satisfactory legal mortgage therefore the bank would need to seek Mrs. Mosley's agreement, with independent advice, to either postpone whatever rights she may have or charge them in favour of the bank. This situation is now a very real factor to allow for when taking residential properties as security (*Williams & Glyn's Bank Ltd. v. Boland* (1979)) and most banks have amended their procedures to accommodate it. Nevertheless, the important thing is (as in this instance) for the banker to recognise when the need to accommodate the factor exists.

Answer 47

In order to facilitate the deeds being transferred into the name of Mrs. Henshall, it will be necessary to pass the deeds over to the solicitors against their undertaking, and when the property is vested in Mrs. Henshall's name, the bank will need to obtain a new mortgage from her in such a way that it secures Mr. Henshall's own indebtedness to the bank and his guarantee given to cover the company's borrowings.

The bank will not want to leave itself in an exposed position and will therefore release the deeds of the house to the solicitors against their good undertaking to hold them to the bank's order, for title to be transferred into Mrs. Henshall's name, and for her to execute a mortgage covering Mr. Henshall's liabilities concurrently upon transfer. The undertaking would further agree to return the deeds and the new mortgage upon completion of the transaction and at that stage the bank can release its earlier mortgage from Mr. Henshall. The Law Society and the Committee of London Clearing Bankers have standard forms of undertaking which have been agreed and the bank would no doubt therefore use its own standard form which would be in the approved form.

The form of mortgage given by Mrs. Henshall should be a third party form of charge (sometimes called a "collateral mortgage") covering Mr. Henshall's liabilities which will therefore secure, not only his own borrowing, but his guarantee liability for the company's account.

Nevertheless, it should be made absolutely clear to Mrs. Henshall that the security she is giving will also secure indirectly the company borrowing through her husband's guarantee and this should be suitably recorded. In any event, the bank must ensure that Mrs. Henshall receives independent legal advice from her solicitors, who will explain the nature of the security to her fully and who will confirm on the charge form that they have so done.

The fact that the security is a matrimonial home raises the "Boland" aspect (*Williams & Glyn's Bank Ltd. v. Boland* (1979)) and it would appear that the bank's existing security may be defective as Mrs. Henshall has not postponed her rights. When the house has been transferred into her name, Mr. Henshall will have "Boland-type" rights and the bank should therefore get him to postpone these in whatever form they have now incorporated into their procedures.

An alternative to the above method, would be for the title to the property to be transferred into Mrs. Henshall's name but subject to the bank's existing mortgage. This would mean that the bank would remain secured, although to overcome the earlier absence of a postponement of "Boland-type" rights, Mrs. Henshall would need to execute an appropriate letter or deed to make the bank's position stronger than it was formerly.

Answer 48

Notice of a second charge bars priority for any advances made after receipt of notice, unless an agreement has been made with the second mortgagee allowing further advances up to a certain amount in priority to his charge or unless the mortgage imposes an obligation to make further advances. This applies even if the banker has agreed verbally or outside the mortgage deed, to allow advances on current account up to a stated limit which has not been reached — *Hopkinson v. Rolt* (1861).

Therefore when the banker receives notice that Bell, who has mortgaged the deeds of his house to the bank, has executed a second charge over the same property, the banker's immediate action will be to stop the account. This will prevent the Rule in Clayton's Case operating to the bank's detriment. *Deeley v. Lloyds Bank Ltd.* (1912).

Having stopped the account, the banker can rely on the security to cover the outstanding overdraft of £13,600.

As regards Bell's letter saying that he intends to draw cheques taking the account up to £16,000 the bank should inform him that cheques will not be paid (unless credits are paid in to cover — the transactions would need to be put through a new account) as Bell, by giving the second charge over the bank's security, has released the bank from any earlier commitment to a higher figure on the strength of existing security.

The bank could, of course, decide to make available an additional facility but any security held or taken for this would rank after the second charge in favour of B. Young.

Section 8
Answers

Answer 49

The lodging of deeds by the customer's father with a request that further time be given to the borrower by the East Bank Ltd., was tantamount to a contract of guarantee *and should, therefore, have been evidenced in writing*: S.4 of the Statute of Frauds 1677. The failure of the Manager to obtain a guarantee placed the bank in a weak position. It is true that the solicitor's contention that there was no consideration can be refuted — the fact that further time was given to the debtor was in itself consideration — but in the absence of any written guarantee it is difficult to see how the bank can enforce the security or even retain it in respect of the debt due from the son. There is no debt due by the father and therefore the deposit of the deeds by him did not constitute an equitable charge.

The bank might attempt to retain the deeds by denying the absence of consideration and by referring to the interview at which the Chief Clerk was present when the deeds were lodged and would doubtless try to rectify the position by obtaining a guarantee and memorandum of deposit over the deeds but if the father was adamant in the line he had taken and still insisted on the return of the deeds it would appear that the bank would have no option but to accede to the request in which case the bank's sole remedy would be against the son.

Answer 50

(a) A guarantor is entitled to have particulars *of his liability* at any time but he is not entitled to inspect the account which he guarantees. If he requests to see a copy of the account he guarantees, the guarantor should be told that it would be a breach of the implied pledge of secrecy given by the bank to the customer when the account was opened if the request was complied with without the debtor's permission. The guarantor should of course, be told the extent of his liability. Most bank forms of guarantee contain a clause whereby the surety agrees to accept the statement of the bank as to the extent of his liability.

(b) In the case of *National Provincial Bank Ltd. v. Glanusk* (1913) where the debtor was using a guarantee for the purposes not contemplated by the guarantor, it was held that there was no duty on the part of the bank to advise the guarantor of the debtor's activities. Nevertheless, in the instance quoted in the question, the banker should try to protect the guarantor's interest by informing the principal debtor that the bank is not prepared to continue the accommodation if it is to be used for gambling purposes. If, owing to these operations, the borrower's position is altering for the worse, the banker should insist that the guarantor be put in possession of the facts on equitable grounds and if necessary the bank should threaten to call in the advance.

Answer 51

Because of the peculiar nature of his liability; i.e. his responsibility for another person's debt, a surety is very favoured at Common Law and is endowed with many rights. For example, if during the currency of the guarantee the debtor is allowed to deal with any of his securities covering the same advance, the guarantor can claim to be released from his liability on the grounds that he is prejudiced by a dealing between the creditor and the principal debtor. Again, if the debtor's position deteriorated and the bank, in common with other creditors, agreed to a composition to save the expense of bankruptcy proceedings, the guarantor would be prejudiced in his rights against the debtor (if he discharged his guarantee liability and chose to find his remedy against the debtor in making him bankrupt he could not do so). Also, if the creditor "gives time" to the debtor by binding contract the guarantor could normally claim to be released from his liability.

In other words, any material alterations in the contract without the guarantor's consent may avoid the contract in the absence of stipulation to the contrary. Therefore a bank must strengthen its position by expressly excluding the guarantor's normal rights by terms inserted in the form of guarantee taken.

It follows that the form of letter suggested by the proposed guarantor in the question, while affording the bank some measure of security, would leave the proposed guarantor nearly all his Common Law rights and would adversely affect the bank in its lending relations with the principal debtor. Moreover, although the letter suggests that the surety would be responsible for any sums due from time to time, by the debtor, the words "up to £1,000" could well be construed as a limitation on the amount *to be lent* and not as a limitation of the *surety's liability* so that if more than £1,000 was advanced the guarantor might contend that the conditions of the guarantee were not fulfilled and the guarantee would then be of no avail. Nor is there any provision that the liability will continue notwithstanding the death or bankruptcy of the principal debtor — points which are specifically covered by a bank's form of guarantee. Also, the limitation in amount, as opposed to a limitation of liability, would adversely affect the bank's position should the borrower become bankrupt.

The proposed request should, therefore, be declined on the grounds that such a letter might later cause embarrassment both to the bank and to the guarantor and if the proposed guarantor still refuses to sign the bank's form of guarantee the borrower should be asked to find other security.

In any event, in accordance with modern practice the banker would almost certainly (indeed this instance calls for it particularly) insist on the prospective guarantor seeking independent legal advice which would give the proposed guarantor every opportunity to have all the guarantee clauses explained fully to him.

Answer 52

In this situation the banker is banker to both customer and prospective guarantor and therefore the case *Lloyds Bank Ltd. v. Bundy* (1975) needs to be considered. The main principle is that enunciated in *Cooper v. National Provincial Bank* (1946) where it was held that there was no duty on a bank to disclose matters to an intending guarantor, but care must be taken not to mislead him, and any questions asked must be answered truthfully; moreover, if the intending guarantor is under any misapprehension, then he must not be allowed to remain in that state. If the correction involves the disclosure of the customer's affairs, then the bank's duty of secrecy comes into the position, and it is necessary to have the customer's authority This does not, however, seem to be the position here, and Mr. Ryder seems to be under the impression that the document he is asked to sign is only of minor importance.

Additionally, his mention of the monies which he owes to Pearson gives the impression that he somehow thinks that when he has paid these monies his guarantee would be set aside. It should therefore be explained fully and carefully to Ryder exactly what liability he would be taking on under the guarantee and the bank really should not contemplate accepting a guarantee from him, other than one which has been fully explained to him by his solicitor, and certified to that effect.

Answer 53

The question of how a banker should deal with cheques drawn on a guaranteed account after notice of determination of the guarantee has been received is a difficult one. Bank Forms of guarantee contain a stipulated period of notice which must be given and in this question the appropriate period is three months.

Therefore the bank has the right legally to continue Mr. Raymond's account until the expiration of three months from today and at the end of that period would advise the guarantor of the amount of his liability but in practice the banker would feel it necessary to have some regard for the position of the guarantor.

There are differing views on whether during the three month period, the banker should make fresh advances but many bankers would consider that they have the right to pay cheques presented during the period even if this means increasing the debt or, as would be the case here, letting the account go from a credit balance to a debit one. However, it would be considered right upon receipt of notice from the guarantor, for the banker to consult the customer and the guarantor in order to try to reach some form of arrangement for honouring cheques drawn in respect of commitments entered into by the customer on the strength of the guarantee. If the customer can provide alternative security, or in this case if Mr. Raymond can manage without the overdraft facility, the situation is easily resolved.

Thus the banker should proceed on the above lines but he should (unless Mr. Raymond agrees to cancel the overdraft facility or can provide other satisfactory security) write to the guarantor acknowledging receipt of notice but stating that under the terms of the guarantee three months' notice is the agreed period and therefore the bank will be in a position to advise the guarantor of the amount of the guarantee liability only at the end of that period.

Answer 54

In the absence of any clause to the contrary in the guarantee form, when funds are received from a guarantor in discharge of his liability, they would have to be placed directly in reduction of the debt. (If the funds were stated to be in support, rather than discharge, of the guarantee liability they would be placed in a suspense type account — sometimes known as a "Relief or Realisation" account.)

If, as in the question, the substantiation of the guarantee, does not fully repay the bank, the bank will be at a disadvantage if the monies have been placed in reduction of the debt in the event of the customer's bankruptcy. Bank guarantee forms usually cover this point by providing not only for liability for the whole of the debt but with a supporting statement that the surety will not prove in competition with the bank in the event of bankruptcy and also that until the banker has been satisfied in full the surety will take no steps against the principal debtor in respect of sums paid in discharge of the liability (whether or not bankruptcy ensues).

Thus the banker on receipt of the £800 from Mr. Eaves should credit this to a suspense account, the designation indicating that the funds are received from the guarantor in substantiation of his liability. Interest would not run against the guarantor and the bank would no doubt in its books set-off *for interest purposes* the £800 against the "first" £800 of the principal debt.

In any further attempts to obtain recovery from Reynolds, or in the event of bankruptcy, the bank will claim the full debt outstanding of £1,100. In bankruptcy, the bank would therefore receive a dividend on £1,100, whereas had the guarantor's monies been placed directly in reduction of the debt, the bank would be able to prove only for £300 and the bank's recovery would be reduced correspondingly.

Answer 55

(a) If C.D., who guarantees A.B's account for £1,000, supported by a Life Policy for £2,000 on his (the guarantor's) life dies when A.B's account is £750 overdrawn the action which the bank will take in respect of the account will depend on the terms of the guarantee. If the guarantee does *not* contain a clause whereby the guarantor binds his personal representatives, the account should be stopped to prevent the operation of the Rule in Clayton's Case. If, as is more usual, such a clause is contained in the guarantee the account may continue.

(b) Immediately notice of the death of the guarantor is received, the banker should ascertain who are the deceased's personal representatives and take the earliest opportunity of advising them of the existence of the liability and the terms under which it can be determined. An acknowledgment should be obtained. (A point of interest in this respect is that if it transpired that the principal debtor was C.D's executor and deliberately withheld giving notice to determine the guarantee, in order that further advances might be made to him personally, the banker would be wise to call a halt to the advance. It might also be advisable to do so if the banker knew the whole of the guarantor's estate was devised on trust.) It is customary for the personal representatives to give notice to determine the guarantee and at the expiration of that notice; i.e. when the guarantee is determined, the account must be stopped.

(c) With regard to the life policy, the banker should obtain a copy of C.D's death certificate and prove the death with the company concerned by submitting the certificate, the policy, the form of charge and, if any, all other documents of title, to the company. If the company is satisfied that all is in order, payment of the amount due under the policy will be made to the bank who should credit the amount received to a suspense account. When Probate of C.D's will has been granted to the executors, or, if he has died intestate, Letters of Administration have been granted, the bank can release any surplus proceeds to the personal representatives, retaining sufficient to meet the guarantee liability, viz: £1,000.

(a), (b) and (c) A.B. should, of course, be immediately informed of the death of C.D. and should be asked to provide alternative security. If and when he does so, the guarantee can be cancelled and C.D's estate released from liability.

Answer 56

When a banker is to take a guarantee from a company it is essential that he examines the company's Memorandum of Association to make certain that the company has express power to give guarantees.

If the banker is satisfied on this point he should then examine the articles to ascertain in what manner the guarantee may be given. Usually the guarantee can be given under the hand of a duly authorised official of the company but, if the articles require the guarantee to be under seal, then the guarantee must be executed in this way. The fixing of the seal should be witnessed as stipulated in the articles.

It will be necessary to have a certified copy of the Board Resolution authorising the giving of the guarantee and it is important that the Resolution should state that the guarantee is to be in the form and terms of the specimen guarantee put before the Board. This is as a safeguard against the company — or its liquidator if it has failed — at a later stage trying to escape liability under the guarantee on the grounds that the resolution related to a contract of guarantee in general terms and not a guarantee form as taken. It is common practice for the resolution to be endorsed on the actual guarantee document and this practice does, of course, take care of the danger outlined above.

The question states that there are no common directors and therefore the question of "interested directors" (*Victors v. Lingard* (1927)) does not apply. Similarly there are no inter-company shareholdings and therefore it will not be necessary to invite the directors of Avondale to consider whether or not it is in the interests of their company to enter into the proposed guarantee nor for this point to be referred to in the resolution — *Charterbridge Corporation Ltd. v. Lloyds Bank Ltd.* (1969).

Commercial justification would seem clearly to exist as Aston, as Boden's main supplier, stand to gain considerably from the continued trading of Boden.

Section 9

Answers

Answer 57

(a)
- Partners to execute bank's general letter of pledge.
- Goods to be inspected.
- Warehousekeeper's warrants to be transferred into name of bank (if only warehousekeepers' receipts offered, further steps are necessary).
- Regular inspection/valuation of goods will be required.
- Ensure adequate insurance cover exists with the bank's interest acknowledged by insurance company.
- Ensure standing of warehousekeeper by status enquiries etc.
- Consider standing of buyer making such enquiries as necessary.
- Remember the high degree of risk inherent in this type of security arrangement.
- Risk increases when goods released by bank; obtain trust letters from the partners to prevent possible claim by trustee in bankruptcy under doctrine of ostensible ownership.
- Advances should be made by way of loan for each consignment of goods.
- Healthy margin in the "security" should always be sought.
- Integrity of customer who is allowed to sign a trust letter is of paramount importance.
- Contracts of sale, where goods pre-sold, should be examined.

(b) As regards the claim arising from Atlas Financing Ltd., there is a danger that this claim will be upheld. In *Lloyds Bank Ltd. v. Bank of America* (1938) Lloyds Bank made a produce loan to a customer in respect of imported goods; and in due course documents of title arrived at the bank and were released to the customer against his signature on a trust receipt. Instead of using the documents to obtain the goods so that he could sell them and repay Lloyds Bank, the customer pledged them again with another bank — who acted in good faith — and then disappeared. Thus both banks had lent against the same security and the principle held in such a situation was that the party who should lose must be the party whose action made the fraud possible (i.e. Lloyds Bank). The rights of the innocent third party giving value and acting in good faith (Bank of America) must be upheld. However, although in the situation outlined in this question the bank is clearly in a weak position in respect of the claim by Atlas Financing, the bank may have a valid counterclaim against the warehousekeeper for negligence depending upon the facts of the release and this is an aspect which the bank should look into with its legal advisers.

With regard to the German supplier's claim, then clearly the claim is based upon reservation of title — relevant case is *Aluminium Industrie Vaasen BV v. Romalpa Aluminium Ltd.* (1976). The bank should examine the contract and other sale documents in order to try to ascertain the actual terms of trade but, if these included suitably drafted clauses giving the supplier retention of title rights, then the bank would probably lose its security. In practice, the bank should start off adopting a fairly robust resistance to the claim, but may have to concede should examination of the documents reveal a clear retention of title by the German supplier.

Answer 58

Taking the Life Policy as security:
- Read the policy carefully to check no special restrictions.
- Check age admitted (if not, obtain birth certificate).
- Check that wife is named in policy.
- Have legal assignment over policy signed by Mr. Mosley and joined in by his wife (Mrs. Mosley being independently advised by her solicitor).
- Give notice in duplicate to the company, querying existence of any prior charges, whether premiums paid to date (see comments later on arrears) and what official surrender value is.
- Diary for payment of future premiums and maturity (unless company has agreed to advise non-payment of premiums).

Taking the agricultural charge as security:
- Have bank's form of agricultural charge signed by Mosley and witnessed by a bank officer.
- have customer also sign a Form A.C.1 which is the form for registration of the charge at the Agricultural Credits Department.
- Ensure charge registered within seven days of creation.
- After taking the security, search on Form A.C.6 to ensure bank's charge properly recorded (an earlier search would have been made by bank to ensure no prior charges).

Check Mosley's insurance cover regarding stock etc. and give notice of bank's interest to insurance company.

As regards the valuation of these items of security, the bank will need to make further enquiry. The premiums on the life policy are apparently in arrears and the effect of this on the surrender value needs to be ascertained by a careful scrutiny of the policy and enquiry to the company. Premium arrears are usually deducted from the surrender value but sometimes a policy becomes void upon non-payment of premiums in which case it would have no value as security. When the position with the arrears has been clarified the bank can decide what steps to take and may insist on Mosley bringing the arrears up to date immediately to restore the full surrender value. A note of the official surrender value (when established on the above lines) should be made in the bank's security records.

The value of the agricultural charge rests on the value of Mosley's assets which will be embraced by the charge and a schedule of these, with the relative values shown, should be noted in the bank's security and lending records. Excluding the life policy which is being separately charged, the value of the agricultural charge based on Mosley's own draft figures (the bank should visit the farm and satisfy themselves with his figures — periodic visits should be arranged thereafter) would be £115,110 i.e. Total assets less life policy and debtors and deducting also the preferential creditor for tax.

Section 10

Answers

Answer 59

The first thing which is apparent here is that there has been considerable carelessness since the cheque in (iii) is post dated and should therefore have been returned yesterday, as should the cheque in (v) which is out of date. The cheque drawn in accordance with the cheque card scheme would in any event have to be paid provided it was drawn fully in accordance with the rules, which seems to be the case. The rules for the late return of cheques are agreed between the members of the London Bankers' Clearing House, and the inadvertance rule is that a cheque may be returned on the day following presentation by reason of a shortage of funds or countermand of payment. There is no agreement that cheques which were technically out of order can be returned and consequently those cheques which were "out of date" and "post dated" could not be returned under the inadvertance rule unless they were also being returned for lack of funds (i.e. "Refer to Drawer"). Therefore the clerk should be told to contact the presenting banks and seek their agreement to accept as late returns the cheques in (i), (iii) and (v), in the case of (iii) and (v) stating that the cheques are being returned "Refer to Drawer" due to shortage of funds whilst the cheques are both technically defective also. Under the late return rules, it is agreed that where a cheque is over £50 the returning branch will telephone the presenting bank before 12 noon, and the bank officers who speak to each other in the respective banks should exchange names and make a note of these. The direct debit can be returned and the appropriate answer is "Refer to debtor" but on a practical note it would be wise to check to see if the item relates to a premium on a policy which is part of the bank's security since, if so, the premium should perhaps be paid to preserve this item of security.

As regards the £100 cheque now presented over the counter, this can be unpaid and Mr. Moore can be told that the cheque is not paid. There is no need to wait until the close of business before giving the answer — in *Ringham v. Hackett* (1980) the judge clearly recognised the right of a payee to an answer in such circumstances it not being necessary for a crossed cheque to be presented through a banker.

Answer 60

- The bank's debenture will contain a clause precluding company from creating fixed charge which would rank in priority or *pari passu* to floating charge.
- The above clause will have been registered at Companies Registration Office — notice to the world.
- As Topline Funding are to have a fixed charge, they will want the bank to agree by way of letter of priority. (This is usually a deed between three parties: the company, the factors and the bank.)
- It may retain certain rights over debts for the bank after the factors are paid.
- Obtain an undertaking from the factors to remit funds direct to the bank.
- Basically, the bank will lose the value of its floating charge over debtors.
- It may therefore wish to review the extent of its lending, especially as the factors will pay to the company against outstanding debtors on a regular (monthly) basis.

Answer 61

The bank is at present satisfactorily secured for the overdraft but this will not automatically be the case when the borrowing is taken in the name of Hallows (Mark II) Ltd. At present the bank has an unlimited debenture which embraces both the fixed and current assets but this will not extend to any assets of the new company.

The question does not say what happens to the existing current assets and liabilities at the beginning of next month — they could remain with Hallows Ltd. or be transferred into the new company. However, if they are not transferred it is only a matter of time before the current assets to which the bank will be looking for security cover will be in the new company (since that company is to take over the trading) and therefore a debenture from Hallows (Mark II) Ltd. needs to be taken. The question does not indicate what is happening to the property, which is an important part of the security but presumably it is staying in the existing company who are already charging it to the bank. This can therefore easily be made available as security under the new arrangement by taking a guarantee (either for £100,000 or in unlimited form) from the existing company in favour of the new one. The question of whether the value of the freehold would be affected if Hallows (Mark II) Ltd. occupies the property should be considered. The question refers to the borrowing in future being taken by the new company but to give maximum flexibility, the bank could suggest that unlimited cross-guarantees be taken between the two companies which would mean that the overdraft facility could if desired be made available on a "group" basis between the two companies. In any event, there is undoubtedly to be a trading relationship between the two companies and therefore due consideration for the giving of the guarantee.

As regards the debenture to be given by the new company, Section 322 of the Companies Act 1948 (now Section 617 of the 1985 Act) should be considered although it seems unlikely that the question of insolvency arises; however an opening "pro forma" balance sheet of Hallows (Mark II) Ltd. could be obtained to demonstrate the bank's prudence on this point.

The following steps will be necessary:

The Guarantee — Ensure that the existing company has the power to give a guarantee by examining its memorandum of association (and that the new company is similarly empowered if cross-guarantees are to be taken). Borrowing powers of this company should have previously been checked in view of the existing borrowing.

SECTION 10: ANSWERS

Ensure that the guarantee is executed in accordance with the articles of association and an appropriate resolution obtained.

The Debenture — Obtain the Memorandum and articles of the new company and the certificate of incorporation. Check that the proposed borrowing is within the company's and directors' powers and is *ultra vires* the objects of the company. If the bank wishes to impose a formula with which it will monitor its debenture cover, this should be agreed and will in due course be stated in the bank's facility letter. A search should be made at Companies House and the debenture should be executed in accordance with the company's articles and registered at Companies House within 21 days (Section 95 Companies Act 1948 — now Section 395 of the 1985 Act). The bank should check that insurance of stock is adequate and effected in the name of the new company, and give notice to the insurance company. By making these arrangements, the bank will then remain fully covered for the proposed borrowing.

Answer 62

There are three inherent problems which make the proposed security unattractive for the bank. There would seem to be no commercial justification for Valex Nurseries Ltd. to undertake obligations on behalf of Drax Micro Ltd. — Re *Charterbridge Corporation v. Lloyds Bank* (1969) is relevant here. The other two problems concern the valuation of the land. Clearly it is in agricultural use and as such might not be readily saleable in a realisation situation. Further, whilst it can be charged if it is in the name of Mr. Vernon, even so Valex Nurseries Ltd. must have rights of occupancy either under a formal tenancy, informal tenancy or by virtue of the Boland decision, and the bank could therefore find itself with a virtually worthless security, being unable to evict Valex Nurseries Ltd.

The following sets out the drawbacks in tabulated form:

Guarantee by Valex Nurseries Ltd.

- Almost certainly a defective security.
- Even if specific power to give guarantees was present in the Memorandum of Association.
- No commercial justification for such an obligation being undertaken by a director on the company's behalf.
- No benefit to Valex Nurseries Ltd. — Charterbridge Case.
- The company mortgage in support of the guarantee would be void for the same reasons.

If the land were in the name of Mr. Vernon:

- He could give a third party charge, which would be good legally.
- Valuation would be important and it could have agricultural value only.
- Could land be sold to repay bank if necessary?
- Valex Nurseries Ltd. would seem to have a tenancy — formal or otherwise — and the bank's mortgage would be subject to that tenancy.
- Valex Nurseries Ltd. might also have protection under Agricultural Acts.
- The bank could not sell with vacant possession.

Answer 63

Company's leasehold land and buildings

Advantages

Can be good security if reasonable number of years to run and no onerous covenants — ascertain terms.

Would be direct security, thus less open to challenge later.

If long leasehold, good condition and access and multi-purpose or easily adaptable, may be good security from saleability viewpoint — query use/purpose of buildings/planning permission.

Seek professional valuation (forced sale basis).

Disadvantages

Value of security will fall steadily as remainder of term gets less.

There may be a requirement to repair property to certain state etc. just before expiry — chances of negotiating fresh term?

Ground Rent payable.

Would be direct security in liquidation of company — bank therefore would be secured creditor but could not prove for full amount and then resort to the security.

Joint and Several Guarantee by directors

Shows their faith in the business.

Binds them legally to the company's borrowing.

Indirect security in event of company liquidation.

Other than moral value, is only as good as their personal means (primarily here the proposed supporting security).

Despite wording of usual guarantee, there can be considerable dispute in the event of bank calling on both guarantors.

Second Mortgages over the directors' homes

Is "tangible" security.

Query — name/amount of prior mortgage? — can affect bank's view of value of security considerably.

Will be big incentive for directors, not to see the business fail thus jeopardising their homes.

Indirect security in winding up of company.

Not easily realisable — involves eviction maybe, and can be bad for "image." — other mortgagee is involved.

"Boland" aspect — care needed when taking security.

Postponement of Directors' Loans

Shows there is commitment to the company.

In liquidation of company, would not rank equally with bank.

Bank should take a letter of postponement/subordination and an undertaking not to reduce the loan monies.

Bank could also take an undertaking from the Company not to repay the loan monies without consent of bank.

Is not real or tangible security that can be realised.

Only "remedy" if breaches occur would be to sue for breach of contract — probably not of practical value or use at the time.

Answer 64

In *Cuckmere Brick Co. Ltd. v. Mutual Finance Ltd.* (1971) it was held that a mortgagee was not merely under a duty to act in good faith but also to take reasonable care to obtain the true market price at the time he chose to sell.

In *Bank of Cyprus Ltd. v. Gill* (1979) it was held that the bank was not obliged to postpone a sale in anticipation of a rising market. *Barclays Bank Ltd v. Thienel* (1978) concerned a guarantor trying to avoid liability on the argument that an asset of the principal debtor had been sold at too low a price but the guarantor failed, and there was a clause in the guarantee allowing the bank to realise assets of the principal debtor in any way and at any consideration, without affecting the liability of the guarantor. The bank could therefore argue that as it had taken professional advice and could demonstrate that it had acted in a fair and reasonable manner, the company itself would not have been able to claim; nor would the guarantor because of his contract in the guarantee form. The decision in the Thienel case and *Latchford v. Bierne* (1981) which excluded a duty to a guarantor by a mortgagee and, respectively, a receiver were overruled in *Standard Chartered Bank Ltd. v. Walker & Walker* (1982).

In this case it was held that a receiver has to take proper care to obtain the best price. If he seeks professional advice, then he has a defence against any claims of negligence or failing in his duty. A mortgagee undertaking a sale himself has the same obligations. If he does not interfere (i.e. leaves it ostensibly to the receiver) then he has no such obligation and can pursue a guarantee liability as due by Mr. & Mrs. Walker.

This extends somewhat the dictum in the Cuckmere case mentioned earlier. Under the terms of the bank form of guarantee the guarantor would have agreed to pay interest after demand was made upon him, and the fact that he had resigned from the company is not relevant.

If he had wished to determine the guarantee liability, he should have given written notice to the bank in accordance with the terms of the guarantee. It seems clear that Len Hunt is seeking to avoid paying out under the guarantee on any grounds, since it is unthinkable that a bank would have prevented him from taking independent legal advice if he had so wished. In any case, as a businessman and company director he should clearly have understood the nature of his liability when entering into the guarantee. Thus, although he was a customer, the "Bundy" considerations were not really relevant. The bank should therefore adopt a robust stance and give him an ultimatum of say 14 days in which to put forward his proposals, failing which the bank should instruct its solicitors.

Answer 65

Joint and Several Guarantee

Nature:

- it is in writing, and assumes secondary liability, but is also drawn as indemnity (primary liability) in most bank forms.

Advantages:

- Binds the directors personally to their company's borrowing
- Bank may sue either guarantor for full amount owing.
- Easy to take.

Disadvantages:

- Only worth what the directors are worth.
- Not supported here by tangible assets.
- Difficult to realise.
- Disputes common.

Shares

Nature:

- Equitable charge by deposit but without memorandum of deposit charge form.
- *Harrold v. Plenty* (1901).

Advantages:

- Easy to take without documentation.

Disadvantages:

- Shares in private company: difficult to realise, difficult to value.
- Equitable charge: court order for sale required if owner will not co-operate.
- Company might have own lien: no notice given, prior equities.
- Might be difficult to show that shares were lodged to support guarantee as well as security for private borrowing.
- If guarantee called on company failure shares would be valueless anyway.

Life Policy

Nature:

- Equitable charge by deposit.

Advantages:

- Death value £25,000.

Disadvantages:

- Surrender value is important value. Is there any? Is it small?
- Matures only on death.
- Court order for sale required.
- Executors/beneficiaries might dispute or not co-operate to collect death proceeds: adverse publicity.
- No notice to assurance company given.
- Policies of Assurance Act 1867: prohibits note of equitable interests.
- Since lodged in 1976 before guarantee, would not arguably support guarantee unless there was later written or oral advice to this effect with suitable acknowledgement.

Unlisted Security Market

- Shares would no longer suffer from the regular drawbacks attached to private shares since would be capable of sale (albeit in a restricted market) and official valuation by way of current market price.

Answer 66

The paying of cheques against cheques paid in before sufficient time has elapsed for the cheques to be cleared is running a credit risk since, if cheques which were paid in are returned unpaid an overdraft may result. The practice of drawing cheques against uncleared items, where the uncleared items are cheques drawn by the account-holder on an account he has (or one under his control) with another branch or bank, is known as "crossfiring" or "kite flying" and over the years banks have sustained losses where the practice has been adopted deliberately with an intent to defraud. It is therefore important here for the bank to establish whether or not Mr. Beaumont is innocently misusing the clearing system or whether there are more serious and sinister overtones behind his recent actions. If he is innocently drawing against uncleared effects then all the bank needs to do is to explain its unwillingness to allow him to continue the practice and presumably he will do so. Should he genuinely need an overdraft facility, then this is something the bank could consider and go into with him fully. If for some reason the bank will not grant Mr. Beaumont a facility then it certainly must not allow him to draw against uncleared effects since this would leave the bank open to being caught with an overdrawn position if cheques paid in are dishonoured. Where fraudulent schemes involving "crossfiring" are set up, these can be quite complicated and may involve several banks and several different accounts, making detection of the practice much more difficult. Whilst the funds continue to move round, the accounts will remain in funds on uncleared balances, but should a bank return cheques drawn on it, thus breaking the chain, one or more banks could find themselves with losses. The amounts involved in a carefully set up deliberate fraud would usually be fairly substantial. The timing of the discovery that crossfiring is taking place will affect an individual bank or branch involved, since as soon as they become aware of what is going on, they will be faced with either paying or dishonouring cheques drawn against uncleared effects and they are most likely to opt to return the cheques to avoid loss themselves. Obviously on the day in question, the bank concerned would most likely speak to the other banks involved and put them in the picture. Should, however, the bank discovering the fraudulent practice do so at a time when it is waiting for cheques to be cleared, it is of course potentially at risk until the credits are cleared. In such circumstances the bank has to decide whether to inform the other banks of what is going on (or maybe its suspicions) or wait until clearance of the relative cheques which will remove its particular risk. Although by no means certain to indicate crossfiring, an excessive or seemingly excessive turnover on an account in comparison to the size of the business, should be regarded as a warning signal that crossfiring could be taking place, and such a situation ought always to be probed to establish whether or not things are alright.

Answer 67

(i) The banker should of course offer his condolences to Mrs. Gray in her sad bereavement.
- Consider whether necessary to stop account i.e. does bank need to rely on security as if company account overdrawn, Clayton's Case will operate so that future credits will repay existing debt and future debits create a fresh debt, unsecured by the guarantee.
- If necessary, stop account and open a new account for the company and keep it in credit, unless the company's own worth justifies the borrowing or alternative security is available — interview other director(s)/Mrs. Gray as soon as possible, and ask if another director is to be appointed — a new mandate will be required.
- Ask for sight of death certificate in due course.
- Obtain death maturity forms from the life assurance company.
- Complete and submit the claim, with the life policy, charge and death certificate.
- Obtain the £20,000 and credit a suspense account.
- The surplus can be made available to executor/administrator against production of probate/letters of administration.

(ii)
- Continue the account, provided reliance on the guarantee is not required.

- The life policy is a company asset, and monies can be collected as above and will be credited to the company's account.
- Discuss whether an overdraft will therefore be necessary in the future.

Answer 68

Section 319 of the Companies Act 1948 (now contained in Section 614 of the Companies Act 1985) makes provision for any sums advanced by a third party (which includes a bank) for the purpose of payment of wages or salaries of employees of the company during the 4 months prior to liquidation, or the appointment of a receiver, to rank as preferential up to a maximum sum per employee — the maximum sum is now £800 — Insolvency Act 1976. A bank can therefore gain protection if it can identify the amount paid out by way of wages and salaries and the operation of a separate account enables a bank to identify more easily this amount. Advances made for wages and salaries through a current account would equally be preferential but if wages/salaries are debited to the current account, due to the operation of the Rule in Clayton's Case, subsequent credits will go to extinguish wage payments which means that the amount for which the bank can claim preferentially may well be less than it would have been had a separate wages account been operated. With a wages account, the bank will, in the event of liquidation or receivership, rank alongside other preferential creditors such as V.A.T., the Inland Revenue, and National Insurance, for sums advanced for wages up to the amount of its unsecured claim. In this instance, the bank has direct security which may fetch £30,000. Such proceeds could be appropriated to repay the non-preferential debt whilst the bank retains its claim against the liquidator for the money outstanding on the wages account. In practice, the liquidator may well not accept the full amount claimed by the bank and may be able to show that the cheques cashed through the wages account included some amounts for purposes not given preference under Section 319 e.g. petty cash, sums due under PAYE and National Health or payments to directors who are not employed in another capacity. Redundancy payments are not preferential and, unless found by the government under its legislation, would rank with unsecured creditors. A bank may find itself at a disadvantage in respect of the balance in the wages account at the time of liquidation, where the Department of Employment becomes involved in paying salaries/wages under the Employment Protection (Consolidated) Act of 1978. Under this legislation, the Department effectively guarantees an employee his earnings up to a maximum of £130 per week for eight weeks giving a total of £1040 of which £800 would rank preferentially. Where this occurs, the Department's claim would be ahead of the bank.

The operation of a separate wages account will require a separate cheque book for the company's use and the bank should obtain a standing order from the customer so that once the account has been running for 4 months, weekly transfers are made from the the company's current account to the wages account to cancel out the oldest wages cheque. Thus, the balance on the wages account never exceeds the period stipulated under the Companies Act. No other credits should be permitted to this account, and the bank should ensure that the sums advanced for this purpose are paid over the counter (ideally) to known representatives of the company. If wages/salaries cheques are to be issued direct to employees from the wages account, then the bank should each time be given a schedule of names and amounts.

SECTION 10: ANSWERS

Case law relative to wages accounts and matters arising therefrom is:

Re *Primrose Builders Ltd.* (1950).

Re *Rampgill Mill Ltd.* (1967).

Re *James Rutherford & Sons Ltd.* (1964).

Re *E.J. Morel (1934) Ltd.* (1961).

If you have any concerns about our products,
you can contact us on
ProductSafety@springernature.com

In case Publisher is established outside the EU,
the EU authorized representative is:
**Springer Nature Customer Service Center GmbH
Europaplatz 3, 69115 Heidelberg, Germany**

Printed by Libri Plureos GmbH
in Hamburg, Germany